CREATING COMMUNITIES OF THE KINGDOM

CREATING COMMUNITIES OF THE KINGDOM

◆New Testament Models
of Church Planting

David W. Shenk ◆ Ervin R. Stutzman
Foreword by Myron S. Augsburger

HERALD PRESS
Scottdale, Pennsylvania
Waterloo, Ontario

LIBRARY OF CONGRESS
Library of Congress Cataloging-in-Publication Data
Shenk, David W., 1937-
    Creating communities of the kingdom : New Testament models of
church planting / David W. Shenk and Ervin R. Stutzman.
        p.   cm.
    Bibliography: p.
    Includes index.
    ISBN 0-8361-3470-2
    1. Church development. New. 2. Evangelistic work. 3. Bible.
N.T.   Acts—Criticism, interpretation, etc.   I. Stutzman, Ervin R.,
1953-   .   II. Title.
BV652.24.S48 1988
250—dc19   88-11235

The paper used in this publication is recycled and meets the minimum
requirements of American National Standard for Information Sciences—
Permanence of Paper for Printed Library Materials, ANSI Z39.48-1984.

Figure 9-1 on page 159 is taken from *Evangelism Canada,* September
1985. Used by permission of publisher. Except as otherwise indicated,
Scripture quoted is from the *Holy Bible: New International Version* ®.
Copyright © 1973, 1978, 1984 by the International Bible Society. Used
by permission of Zondervan Bible Publishers. All rights reserved.
Copyright clearance information for this book is on page 6.

CREATING COMMUNITIES OF THE KINGDOM
Copyright © 1988 by Herald Press, Scottdale, Pa. 15683
    Published simultaneously in Canada by Herald Press,
    Waterloo, Ont. N2L 6H7. All rights reserved
Library of Congress Catalog Card Number: 88-11235
International Standard Book Number: 0-8361-3470-2
Printed in the United States of America
Design by Gwen M. Stamm

04 03 02   10 9 8 7 6 5

To order or request information, please call
1-800-759-4447 (individuals); 1-800-245-7894 (trade).
Website: www.mph.org

To

David's father, J. Clyde Shenk,

*who has been a 20th-century model
of biblical church planting during 40 years
of pioneer evangelism in East Africa*

and

Ervin's father, Tobias Stutzman,

*who went to be with the Lord when
Ervin was only three, but whose life
modeled faithfulness to Christ.*

Contents

Foreword

To be the church is to be in mission, for the church is the body of Christ, the Savior. This study on church planting in the book of Acts helps us to understand the first-century church in its mission. St. Luke traces the spread of the church from Jerusalem across Asia Minor and on to Rome. He does not share the whole story of its spread across North Africa, but he does show us the dynamics of the movement. This people of the way—described by Paul as a third people (1 Cor. 10:32)— are above all disciples of Jesus Christ.

The book of Acts, the acts of the Holy Spirit, gives enriching insight into Christian faith and mission. Viewed in relation to church planting, it brings a specific focus to our understanding which is especially meaningful as a guide in new ventures of church development. We are indebted to the coauthors for some fresh and practical thinking on biblical guidelines for mission.

Stutzman and Shenk, both deeply engaged in mission and ministry, come from very different backgrounds. One grew up in the Midwest of the United States, while the other grew up in Tanzania in a missionary family and later served in East Africa himself as a missionary. Each brings different insights and illustrations to his writing which are helpful in the attempt to interpret and contextualize the message of reconciliation.

Creating Communities of the Kingdom speaks at a time when there is an increased emphasis on church planting. As we seek the Lord's guidance in developing congregations of disciples in every community possible, we need to study the Holy Spirit's pattern in the book of Acts. Here we find the keys for interpretations, contextualization, and innovation in a variety of cultural contexts. We are not a franchise church, identical in every situation. Each congregation as the body of Christ allows the context to shape its expression. With the increased urbanization and pluralism of worldwide society, the church planter needs a security in Christ and his Word that provides the freedom for a creative and innovative ministry.

As I read this stimulating study I was reminded of the words of Theodore Wedel: mission includes presence, service, and communication. As agents of reconciliation we need to be a presence for Christ wherever we are placed. We need to serve people as they need to be served, not as we prefer to serve them. We need to communicate those things which we believe about the lordship of Christ.

The authors of this book are especially helpful to those committed to being a believers church which provides a special freedom in sharing the message of reconciling love. I join them in emphasis and in prayer that each reader will be challenged to be a more effective ambassador for Christ.

—*Myron S. Augsburger*

Introduction

Fatima and her husband are immigrants to the United States from Senegal, West Africa. They moved to Lancaster County, Pennsylvania, and were quickly traumatized by the required cultural adjustments. Deeply depressed, Fatima decided to put an end to her life. She went to a drugstore, purchased some pills, and then slipped into the local laundromat to wash her family's clothes for the last time. According to her plans, this would be her final day on earth.

While in the laundromat, a joyful little Hispanic woman who knew little English stepped briskly into the laundromat and handed Fatima a tract. That was all. The Hispanic woman vanished outside while Fatima peered at the tract, astonished. It said, "You need Jesus, not pills." She read the crumpled piece of paper with tears trickling down her auburn cheeks. She experienced the conviction of the Holy Spirit. Leaving the laundromat with her newly washed clothing, she was surprised to see the Hispanic woman standing on the street corner. With broken English the Hispanic woman asked Fatima, "Did you read paper? Do you believe Jesus?"

Fatima, with joy, threw her arms around that little Hispanic woman and sobbed. "Yes, I read your tract and I have decided to believe in Jesus."

Fatima searched for a church, and found a local Mennonite congregation. It was there that she confessed her faith in Jesus and began a yearlong study of the Bible. She discovered with surprise the marvelous story of God's saving acts among people. Fatima and her husband had always been Muslims. For them, it was an amazing discovery to learn that God is the loving heavenly Father who invites people to become his sons and daughters. In preparation for the Sunday of Fatima's baptism, she sent printed invitations to all her friends, but she was not able to locate the little Hispanic woman to whom she owed her life and that first glimpse of the way of salvation.

This book is written with the same sense of urgency that the Hispanic woman revealed when she shared that tract with Fatima in the laundromat. We firmly believe that the greatest favor anyone can ever do for another person is to share Jesus.

Four questions set the tone for this study:

1. Should everyone in your community have the opportunity to say "yes" to Jesus?

2. Has everyone in your community been introduced to Jesus with sufficient clarity and attractiveness that he or she can say "yes" to him?

3. Is your congregation making sure that everyone in your community is having the opportunity to say "yes" to Jesus?

4. Is your congregation helping to share the gospel with at least some other communities, including some of the 16,000 groups of people around the world who have never heard the gospel?

There are two ways in which we who are part of the church of Jesus Christ extend the evangelistic invitation. One is through the prayer, life, and ministry of an established congregation reaching out into the community and inviting people to come to faith in Jesus. The second way is to plant new congregations who draw into membership those persons who have only recently responded to Jesus. The church needs to be equally committed to both approaches to sharing the gospel.

Nevertheless, the approach accented in the book of Acts is the creation of new congregations. At the time of the apostles and also in our modern age, most of the people who have never believed in Jesus Christ will only respond to the gospel when a new church springs up in their community. This book is a study of how those new churches were planted during the apostolic period in order to help us understand how the approaches to church planting used by the apostles are helpful for us today.

We believe that the Spirit of God is nudging every established congregation to help create sister churches in communities, both nearby and in distant places. We believe that the book of Acts describes how we can do that. It is with that conviction we are writing this book.

This book consists of thirteen chapters and can be used as a weekly study for one quarter of the Sunday school year. All who desire to understand the worldwide mission of the church will benefit from this book. It is ideally suited for a Sunday school class or a midweek study. It is of vital significance for any interest group considering church planting. This book will also be helpful for college or seminary students of missions, evangelism, and church planting. It weaves biblical perspectives into the insights of contemporary theology, anthropology, sociology, psychology, and communication theory. Persons involved in or considering church planting will also benefit from this study. Each chapter weaves together biblical commentary and practical applications to the church today. In most chapters, the topic is examined from:

1. The Acts
2. The Gospels
3. The Epistles

The Bible study leads us to understand the perspectives of the apostles and Jesus and gives examples of biblical approaches in the new churches. The practical applications in each chapter draw from modern sociological insights and approaches to church planting, in the light of the biblical study. Each chapter concludes with questions for review, study, and discussion along with a list of resources for further help. In addition, some chapters have a section challenging the reader to specific action.

The Scriptures we shall study are a call to action. May the Spirit of God enlighten all of us as we consider Jesus' call: Follow me and I will make you fishers of men and women.

Acknowledgments

For a lifetime the authors have moved and lived among church planters. Faithful creators of new congregations have provided for the authors models of faithful witness which they describe in this book. The authors have lived and worked with church planters in Kansas, Ohio, Pennsylvania, New York, Tanzania, Kenya, and Somalia. Their responsibilities in mission administration placed them in intimate contact with hundreds of church planters across North America, as well as in the other five continents and the islands of the seas. We cannot name all these persons to whom we are indebted!

Several pastors, church planters, and teachers of missiology invested in this effort through specific counsel and critique of the developing manuscript. These include Lawrence Yoder, Lindsey Robinson, Henry Schmidt, Marlin Miller, Leon Schnupp, Richard Landis, David Kniss, Peter Wagner, Glen Yoder, and Roger Hughes.

Rita Lentz Wenger and Joyce Swartz invested hundreds of hours typing and retyping the manuscript. Jonathan Shenk assisted in editing. We are indebted to the Eastern Mennonite Board of Missions and Charities, where we work. It has provided for us continuing relationships with newly forming congregations among some seventy language groups in North America and around the world. Eastern Board encouraged the writing of this book and provided time for the authors.

Our spouses, K. Grace Shenk and Bonnie Stutzman, encouraged us continuously. So also have our children.

The two local kingdom communities in which David and Ervin are covenant members also contributed significantly to this effort. The rhythm of worship, fellowship, discipling, ministry, and community under the lordship and saviorhood of Jesus Christ is central to all that we believe and are. These congregations, Mountville Mennonite and Mount Joy Mennonite, are precious contributors to our perspectives.

—David W. Shenk and Ervin R. Stutzman

CREATING COMMUNITIES OF THE KINGDOM

Chapter 1

The Church with the Message

Acts 2:14-41

For ten days, 120 disciples of Jesus had been together in central Jerusalem. They prayed, fasted, and waited for the promised Holy Spirit. Then on Pentecost, the Holy Spirit from heaven filled the whole house where the disciples were staying. They were anointed with power to proclaim the gospel.

As the people in Jerusalem heard what was happening, they ran excitedly toward the house. Thousands upon thousands of people gathered around the disciples, who were praising God with uninhibited joy. Many of the people were from surrounding nations and, miraculously, they heard the disciples telling the marvelous acts of God in the native language of each person! The throngs were "exceedingly amazed."

All the people heard the Word of God in their own language. This was a sign from God that the gospel is intended for all peoples of every culture. As people respond to the gospel, they are united together in a new community. The divisions of Babel were reversed in Pentecost! The church is the new com-

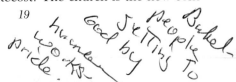

munity which brings healing to the divisions of humankind. Although language and cultural differences never disappeared at Pentecost, people discovered the precious unity and fellowship of the Holy Spirit which brings people of different cultures together as true brothers and sisters.

Preaching the Gospel

Nevertheless, the new community happens only as people respond in faith to Jesus Christ. The response to Christ becomes possible as the disciples of Jesus proclaim with clarity the truth of the gospel. It is not enough to stand in awe of the marvels of the work of the Holy Spirit in the lives of Christians. It was not enough for the thousands gathered on Pentecost to go home proclaiming the event. It was not enough to be "exceedingly amazed." No, a response or commitment to Christ was needed before the people could go home as Christians. That response became possible when Peter preached with the power of the Holy Spirit.

Peter's sermon, as recorded in Acts chapter 2, is the first Christian sermon ever preached. In several key ways, it is a model sermon which sets the tone for all subsequent preaching of the gospel. The simple fact that he stood, rather than following the traditional custom of sitting to teach, has been a pattern for Christian preachers to this day. The preacher stands to proclaim the gospel, often from a pulpit. This is a sign that the gospel is the Word from God which meets and confronts us, calling for us to respond in repentance and commitment.

Notice that Peter was not alone. He was surrounded by 120 other Spirit-filled believers. The eleven other apostles were standing with him, probably nodding approval as he preached. The support of the other believers was important for several reasons: (1) It showed that Peter was not crazy. (2) It helped to make Peter courageous. (3) It provided a prayer base. (4) It was a visual revelation of the communal nature of the church and the new life in Christ.

Note the sermon content. First, Peter began by speaking to the present situation. He reminded them of the recent events in Jerusalem and interpreted the meaning of the signs which accompanied the infilling of the Holy Spirit. In other words, the message was contextually appropriate. Second, the sermon was rooted in Scripture. Peter quoted from the inspired writings of Joel and David in the proclamation of the gospel. It is as though Peter had the newspaper in his left hand and the Scriptures in his right hand. He proclaimed the truth of Scripture in the current situation. Third, he proclaimed Jesus Christ crucified and risen to be Lord and Messiah.

In summary, we can say that Peter's message was contextual, scriptural, and Christ-centered. To say it another way, Peter's message was appropriate to the situation, grounded in Scripture, and centered in Christ.

The consequence of Peter's proclamation was conviction. As Jesus Christ was being proclaimed, the Holy Spirit convicted the people. As the Holy Spirit began to convict, Peter invited people to repent. In fact, he urged them with many words. All Christian preaching needs to be oriented toward inviting people to decision. The decision involves turning away from self-centered living to following Jesus Christ. Christian preaching calls people to repentance, to conversion.

Repentance is unique to biblical faith. Other religions and ideologies do not call for repentance. This is because they are characterized by ethnocentricity. That is, they are rooted in the surrounding culture. They simply call for persons to act according to the cultural, national, or tribal norm. But all truly Christian preaching calls for repentance, a turning away from cultural ethnocentricity to a commitment to Jesus Christ as Lord and Savior. Jesus is always to some extent the stranger in every culture. This is the reason all disciples of Jesus must repent. They need to turn away from the false gods of culture in order to follow Jesus.

Of course not only are the gods of culture false, it is also wrong to live a self-centered life. In our selfishness we are like the modern young person who said that for her, god is the little voice inside of her who says, "Treat yourself as well as possible." But the gospel is the good news that only Jesus is Lord. In repentance we turn away from a self-centered life to follow Jesus Christ.

Three thousand people responded to the evangelistic invitation that day. They repented and were baptized. Then began the great teaching ministry of the church as these persons were taught the meaning of Christian discipleship.

The Kingdom of God

Acts 1:1-3; 28:23, 31

The book of Acts begins and ends with references to the kingdom of God. Peter's sermon was a proclamation of the breakthrough of the kingdom of God. In the words of the prophet Joel, Peter preached: "In the last days, God says, I will pour out my Spirit on all people" (Acts 2:17). There are other references to the kingdom in the book, especially with regard to Paul's preaching. This emphasis on the kingdom in Acts is in harmony with the entire life and ministry of Jesus. After he rose from the dead, he appeared to his disciples over a period of forty days, speaking to them about the kingdom of God. In so doing, he continued the pattern which he had practiced in the three years of ministry with his disciples. Many of his parables, for example, were given to illustrate truths about the kingdom of God. He instructed the twelve to pray for the kingdom to come (Matthew 6:10) and to "seek first his kingdom" (Matthew 6:33).

The apostles were absolutely convinced that Jesus was the fulfillment of God's promises to send the Messiah, the Anointed One to rule the world. This belief provided the framework for their understanding and interpretation of the Old Testament Scriptures. Especially when preaching to the Jewish people, the apostles proclaimed Jesus as the fulfillment of God's promises to establish his kingdom on earth.

The preaching of the good news of Jesus must be woven into the concern for the kingdom of God—the rule of God. The gospel is not just "good news"; it is the "good news of the kingdom" (Matthew 4:23). The good news is that God's rule is being established on earth. His righteousness, justice, love, and grace are demonstrated through Jesus and his followers! What could be better news than that?

The kingdom of God becomes visible in any community whenever a cluster of people gather in Jesus' name. Jesus Christ said, "For where two or three come together in my name, there am I with them" (Matthew 18:20). Elsewhere the apostolic writers frequently refer to the church as "the body of Christ." God's intention is that every congregation of believers in Jesus be a surprising revelation of the presence of the kingdom of God on earth. These surprising colonies of heaven are audiovisual expressions of the continuing life and ministry of Jesus in his fullness in an evil world (Ephesians 1:22-23).

Church planting is thus the most urgent business of humankind. It is through the creation (or planting) of churches that God's kingdom is extended into communities which have not yet been touched by the precious surprise of the presence of the kingdom of God in their midst. Of course all congregations experience sinfulness and failure. Yet whenever the people gathering in Jesus' name repent, a new thing happens. The transforming grace of God recreates the visible presence of the kingdom of God in that cluster of people who are committed to Jesus Christ as Lord and Savior.

The Name of Jesus
Acts 2:38; 3:6; 4:12; 15:26

The apostles were enthralled with the name of Jesus. It was in his name that they preached, baptized, healed, cast out demons, and risked their lives. So confident were they of their message that Peter declared to his opposers, "Salvation is found in no one else, for there is no other name under heaven given to men [and women] by which we must be saved" (Acts 4:12). Even after being jailed, flogged, and forbidden by the Sanhedrin to teach about Jesus, the apostles continued teaching. They rejoiced "because they had been counted worthy of suffering disgrace for the Name" (Acts 5:41).

Certainly, the apostles did not consider the use of the name of Jesus to be a magical formula for success. And yet, a tremendous power was released upon using his name. What was it about the name of Jesus that brought such urgency and power to the preaching of the apostles? Surely they were acting on the promise of Jesus recorded in John 14:14: "You may ask for anything in my name, and I will do it."

The apostles, for the most part, were uneducated men. In a worldly sense, they had few resources at their disposal. But they soon discovered that Jesus had all the resources of heaven and earth at his disposal. Under the authority of Jesus, they became instruments of God's grace, so the good news of the kingdom spread far and wide.

The Ministry of the Holy Spirit
Acts 1:8; 2:38; 9:17

As the apostles preached, they expected the Holy Spirit to be at work in those who heard the message. Occasionally they made reference to the work of the Spirit in their sermons. More often, the Holy Spirit came upon new believers after they responded in obedience to the message. The writer of Acts also refers to occasions when the apostles prayed for persons to receive the Holy Spirit. See, for example, Acts 8:15 and Acts 19:1-7.

Without the ministry of the Holy Spirit, the early church would have been powerless. Knowing this, Jesus commanded his disciples to wait in Jerusalem until the Holy Spirit came.

It was the ministry of the Spirit which convinced Peter that the Gentile household of Cornelius was indeed acceptable to

God. In argument against the Jewish brothers, reluctant to accept these Gentile outsiders, Peter said, "If God gave them the same gift as he gave us, who believed in the Lord Jesus Christ, who was I to think that I could oppose God!" Good reasoning!

Call for Obedience

Acts 2:38; 3:19; 7:51-53

The preaching of the kingdom of God and the good news of Jesus Christ cannot leave people unaffected. The preaching of the apostles, coupled with miraculous signs, prompted people to make a decision. Most often, they called for belief and repentance. Those who responded were baptized.

Many people in the church today have had their ears dulled by preaching which does not call for any commitment. As a result, we have become a generation of hearers, without a sense of urgency to respond to the message. We need a restoration of apostolic preaching which calls for radical change as a result of hearing the Word of God. A church planter cannot expect to build a church with people who make no response to the Word. Healthy growth comes only as persons respond in obedience to the gospel and commit themselves to living under God's rule.

Confident Witness

Acts 1:1-11

The gospel of the kingdom which Peter and the other apostles proclaimed was not a myth, a legend, or wishful thinking. No indeed! The Christian gospel is not philosophical or ideological, which is the case in Hinduism, Buddhism, Marxism, or Islam. In contrast, the Christian faith is historical. It springs out of a faith response to God's acts in history, and supremely, his acts in Jesus.

Because of the historical nature of Christian faith Luke was concerned to accurately record the acts of God within the experience of the early church, as well as in the biography which he wrote of the life of Jesus. (See Luke 1:1-4.) In the opening verses of Acts, Doctor Luke summarizes the acts of God in Christ as including: (1) the works of Jesus; (2) the teachings of Jesus; (3) the sufferings of Jesus; (4) the resurrection of Jesus, and his appearance following the resurrection; and (5) the ascension of Jesus to heaven. These are the five foundation stones of all biblical preaching about Jesus the Christ.

The faithful church proclaims with confidence Jesus Christ of the Scriptures, in all his fullness. The truth of the proclamation of Jesus of the Scriptures is further demonstrated by Christian experience. The work of the Spirit of Christ in the life of the believer assures us that Jesus is all that he claimed to be. This is to say that Christian experiences and the historical salvation events of the past are complementary. Both are evidences of the truth of the gospel. We, therefore, may give witness with confidence and joy.

With humility, confidence, and power we proclaim the gospel of the kingdom as the truth. "Two plus two equals four" is not a biased statement; it is true. If we can state with confidence the truth of something as comparatively inconsequential as the tally of numbers, with more urgency and confidence we proclaim Jesus who said, "I am the truth." Happily for all believers, Jesus needs no defense. He needs witnesses, but not defenders, for he is his own defense.

The gospel includes promise. The disciples wondered when the kingdom would be restored. Jesus did not attempt to resolve their perplexity about the political disorders of the day. Rather, he encouraged them to walk in faith, confident that God in his own time and way would fulfill his purpose in history. So the gospel is also a promise that God will bring about the consummation of his kingdom at the conclusion of history.

By faith, we know that God will fulfill his promises. This promise of future fulfillment cannot be proved or demonstrated in quite the same way as the crucifixion or resurrection of Christ can be demonstrated. Yet we rest in the confidence that God, who has so faithfully fulfilled his promises in

the past, will also fulfill his promise concerning the fulfillment
of the kingdom.

The Church in Pilgrimage

Acts 7:1-8

In his defense before the Sanhedrin, Stephen reminded his
hearers that Abraham was called to leave the evil cultural
practices of Haran and begin a pilgrimage of faith toward a
land he had never seen. His life, his values, and his culture
were to be transformed in obedience to the principles of the
righteousness of God, with the promise of God's blessing. In a
similar way, the church is constantly in pilgrimage, moving
from what it is to what God is calling it to become in obedience
to Jesus the Lord. The Christian is always somewhat uneasy
within the cultural and historical situation. It is obvious that the
kingdom of God is never in full harmony with human society.
The pilgrim church resists the pressures of the surrounding evil
culture. We are pilgrims facing the eschaton, the eventual
fulfillment of the kingdom of God.

Even though the church at times experiences persecution,
the journey is not one of sadness. Always, in all circumstances,
there is a touch of joy because we are confident that at the
climax of history, the lordship of Jesus will be firmly established
over all creation and humankind.

The Evangelistic Invitation

Acts 26

The Christian pilgrimage is the story of a movement which
begins when a person experiences conversion by saying "yes"
to Jesus Christ. Even in the presence of kings and authorities
Paul did not hesitate to give verbal witness to his conversion
and the new life in Christ. He even invited the king to respond
in faith to Jesus.

The church is a community of converted people, on a
journey of obedience to Jesus Christ. These believers give faith-

ful witness to the new life they have experienced in Christ, to the presence of the kingdom of God in their midst. They know that salvation is found only through faith in the Lord Jesus Christ. As they journey they invite others, with urgency, to commit their lives to Jesus Christ, to join them in the pilgrimage of life and joy. They eagerly anticipate the eternal fulfillment of the kingdom of God at the climax of history when Jesus returns to earth in glory.

Matthew 28:18-21

Just before Christ's ascension to heaven, he commanded his disciples to be his witnesses in all parts of the world and to make disciples of all nations. At the Pentecost event and in Peter's sermon we see disciples responding in faithfulness to this, the great commission of Jesus, their Lord. Persons from at least a dozen nations seem to have responded to the evangelistic invitation on the day of Pentecost. As disciples of Jesus respond in faithfulness to his Holy Spirit's call, the church experiences continued expansion from person to person, nation to nation, culture to culture, and language to language.

The Kingdom of God Is at Hand

In Philadelphia, Muslims and Christians occasionally meet for dialogue. These meetings sometimes take place in one of the mosques. On one such occasion it seemed that the Christian witness was not being heard. Tension permeated the room and several of the Christians decided to pray silently that the Lord Jesus would be glorified through the conversation. And then, indeed, the spirit of the meeting changed.

After some two hours of conversation, the final question of the evening was presented. "You Christians believe that at the end of history the kingdom of God will be fulfilled. What are you doing about that hope now?"

One Christian responded, "Come visit my church, for in my church you will see the kingdom of God already present."

The Muslims in that mosque determined to visit that church to see and touch and hear and feel for themselves a congregation which is revealing the presence of the kingdom of God.

God's intention is that every Christian church be an authentic revelation of the presence of the kingdom of God. The eschaton has already begun in the community of believers who meet in Jesus' name. That is good news!

Action Challenge

1. Have you said "yes" to Jesus? If not, consider making that commitment right now. If you have said "yes," consider the implications. Are you saying "yes" to all that this commitment implies? Make a list of areas which you desire to surrender to Jesus.

2. Study five of the seven parables in Matthew 13 which Jesus told to illustrate truths about the kingdom. What does each one reveal about the nature of the kingdom of God?

3. Find two sermons recorded in the book of Acts, other than the Acts 2 sermon. What is the central theme of each one? How do they compare to Peter's sermon in Acts 2? Do they have characteristics similar to the four outlined in this chapter?

4. In what ways is your congregation "surprising" your community with the good news? In what ways is your own life and witness a good news surprise to others? Are there fresh ways in which the Holy Spirit desires you or your congregation to be a good news surprise?

For Further Help

The Call to Conversion, by Jim Wallis, Harper and Row, San Francisco, 1981. A description of the broad dimensions of conversion from a New Testament perspective.

Communication Theory for Christian Witness, by Charles H. Kraft, Abingdon Press, Nashville, 1983. A comprehensive study of modern communication theory in the light of biblical revelation.

The Kingdom of God: The Biblical Concept and Its Meaning for the Church, by John Bright, Abingdon Press, Nashville, 1983. A thorough description of the progressive unfolding of the kingdom of God in the Bible.

Chapter 2

Prayer, Call, and Commissioning

Blasio Kigozi was a Christian schoolteacher in Rwanda, Central Africa. He was discouraged by the lack of life in the church and the powerlessness in his own experience. That was in 1935.

Blasio decided to follow the example of the apostolic church, so he closed himself in his little cottage for a week of prayer and fasting. He came from that little room a transformed man—a man on fire with the compassion of Christ. Then he confessed his sins to those he had wronged, including his wife and family. With the simplicity and the power of the Holy Spirit, he proclaimed the gospel in the school in which he was teaching. Most of the student body and faculty community were transformed as the Holy Spirit moved throughout that school with convicting power. Hundreds wept in repentance and were converted.

They were called *abaka*, meaning people on fire. Shortly after that, Blasio was invited to Kampala, Uganda, to share with the leaders of the Anglican church. Again in simplicity,

boldness, and love he called upon them to repent. The fire of
God fell upon that assembled group of leaders. With weeping
and repentance many turned to the Lord.

Several days later Blasio died of fever. His short ministry
lasted only a few weeks. But the fire of revival which the Holy
Spirit lit through his brief ministry has not ceased in East Africa
to the present day. The revival has spread to other continents.
Recently a revival team was invited to minister even in China.
Blasio's experience in prayer was the beginning of the mighty
East African revival through which hundreds of thousands of
lives have been transformed over the decades. All movements
of God always begin with the touch of his grace on the life of a
person or group.

Conversion and Call

Acts 9:1-19

Paul was one such person whom God touched. He did not
intend to become a Christian the day he left Jerusalem to go to
Damascus to arrest and imprison Christians. Not in his wildest
imagination did he dream of meeting Christ on that road to
Damascus. But God took the initiative. He met Paul on that
road and called him.

The call of God to Paul revealed Paul's weakness, humanity,
and sinfulness. He emerged from the encounter a converted,
blind man who was later healed of his blindness by Ananias, a
Christian brother in Damascus. So it is for each of us in our
conversion. We experience in our encounter with Jesus our hu-
manness, our sinfulness, our weakness. We also catch a glimpse
of the astonishing potential of becoming a daughter or son of
the God who has created the universe in all its splendor and
intricate diversity. We discover that he is the one whom we
need, the only one worth following.

Each converted person is called by God to a ministry within
the church. For some that ministry is church planting, an apostolic ministry of extending the kingdom of God beyond the

normal confines of the routines of life. That was God's call to Paul. He clarified that call by revealing to Ananias in Damascus that Paul had been chosen to proclaim the gospel among Gentiles. Paul was to cross the cultural and linguistic barriers of the day so the gospel could be heard by people far away.

All church planters need to be converted people. Each person's conversion story is different, just as the waves that break on an ocean beach show variety. Yet each person's experience always consists of one central fact: Jesus meets the person, calls that person to follow him, and the person responds affirmatively. That is conversion, such as Paul experienced on the Damascus road.

After Paul's conversion and call, he spent many years in preparation for the ministry which God had appointed for him. He spent a number of those years in Arabia and, later, in his home city of Tarsus, where he probably made tents out of Angora goat hide.

It is usually wise for a newly converted person to test his or her walk with Christ before assuming a position of leadership in the church. Personal study of the Word and training through disciplined, pastoral education is necessary for effective ministry.

It is also important for the one called to have an opportunity to observe other Christians in leadership positions who model patterns of effective Christian ministry. For Paul, Barnabas was one such leader.

Praying, Fasting, Listening
Acts 11:22-26; 13:1-3

In fact, it was Barnabas who introduced Paul to the thriving church at Antioch and helped him find a place of leadership within that church. This was a remarkable congregation which brought together into one fellowship persons from European, Asian, and African backgrounds.

The Antioch church was a praying church and a fasting church. It is in prayer that the Holy Spirit is able to reveal to the church his intentions and his call. Many times the Holy Spirit desires to call but no one is listening; there is no congregation ready to respond to his commission. Thus the kingdom languishes and the plan of God cannot be fulfilled.

The Antioch church was a listening church. In prayer and fasting the Holy Spirit spoke with clarity: "Set apart Paul and Barnabas for the work to which I have called them" (NIV). So with great joy and solemnity, the church gathered around the two whom the Holy Spirit had named. They laid hands on them, set them apart, and commissioned them for the task of apostolic ministry of church planting among Gentile peoples. They were sent with the blessing of the church in Antioch.

Commissioning

The commissioning of Paul brought together the call of God upon Paul and the confirmation of that call by the church. At the time of Paul's conversion, God had revealed that this man was his chosen instrument for apostolic ministry to the Gentiles. It was some years later that the church also perceived that call. Now the church was prepared to commission.

One's personal sense of call must be confirmed by the church. Otherwise, two serious problems may arise. First, it might be that the aspiring church planter has ulterior motives. Perhaps the idea to plant a church is of one's own making, and not from the Lord. If the church planting ministry is not God's appointment, the church planter may become quickly discouraged and the effort will not bear lasting spiritual fruit. The second problem is that the church planter needs a praying community to provide encouragement. If the planter is a loner, long-term survival is doubtful. Paul returned to Antioch occasionally for refreshment and retreat. All church planters deserve and need that same kind of home church support.

A commissioning service should be planned for the church

planter. This event brings together the themes of personal call and congregational affirmation. The service will include testimonies from the person or persons being commissioned. The congregation should respond by confirming the call through expressions of affirmation and sharing promises from Scripture. Also, commissioning and prayer are often accompanied by the laying on of hands as a symbol that the church is setting this person or group apart for the apostolic ministry of church planting. The commissioning service is a foundation for continued relationship between the church planter and the sending congregation.

Indeed, prayer, call, and commissioning for apostolic mission always flow together!

Seeking for Laborers
John 4:35-38; Matthew 9:37—10:1; Luke 10:1-2

Jesus informed his disciples that part of their ministry should be one of prayer for God to call laborers. Each of the biblical references above reflects a different year in the three-year ministry of Christ, in the order they are listed. Harvest and labor were consistent themes in Christ's ministry. In the latter two Scriptures, the disciples were instructed to pray for laborers. Without adequate laborers, the harvest could not be brought in. The need for workers was urgent because the harvest was ripe and would rot unless persons moved into the fields to bring the grain in quickly.

Jesus' whole life revealed a sense of urgency. Not only did he move from town to town proclaiming the good news of the kingdom and calling people to repentance, but he also sent out his disciples periodically to extend the kingdom. He called disciples to help in the task. We know most about his call to the twelve, but he called others as well, to train and commission as workers.

In a similar manner the church needs to pray for and seek laborers. David Kniss, a church planter says, "My call to church planting happened during my senior year of high school. I was walking to class when a teacher-pastor joined me on that short walk. He placed his hand on my shoulder said, 'God is calling you to be an evangel of the gospel.' "

David comments, "I didn't know God had called me when I started on that one-minute walk. By the time I had arrived at my class, I knew that the Lord was calling me to be an evangelist and pastor."

Jesus prayed and then called specific people to be evangels, just as Barnabas looked for Paul in Tarsus and brought him to Antioch to help in the evangelistic ministry at that church. Likewise, every pastor, church leader and congregation should be prayerfully seeking and encouraging those whom God may be calling. They need to encourage and endorse that call. Jesus commanded: "Ask the Lord of harvest, therefore, to send out workers into his harvest field" (Matthew 9:38).

There was a rhythm in Jesus' discipling of his apostles. They gathered with him to be taught and to observe him in ministry, then he sent them out to proclaim the gospel also. He taught, he modeled ministry as they observed him, then he sent them out for practical experience. Later, they again gathered around him to share all that had happened. This is leadership formation at its best: vision, prayer, call, teaching, modeling, commissioning, experience, and then reporting.

Living Prayerfully

Luke 6:12-16; Matthew 6:9-13

Jesus himself modeled prayer for the disciples. In fact, he spent all night praying before he took the bold step of calling twelve men to be his apostles. It was after a night of prayer and listening to the mind of his heavenly Father that he called together twelve persons out of the many who were following him. These he commissioned to be apostles—men sent with an urgent mission to proclaim the gospel.

Jesus also took steps to teach his disciples how to pray. In what is often called the Lord's Prayer, he provided an outline which his disciples could use to develop their prayer life. The concerns of the Matthew 6 version of the Lord's Prayer may be outlined as follows:

v. 9, Cultivating intimacy with the Father
v. 10, Declaring the kingdom
v. 11, Developing dependency on the Father's provision
v. 12, Reconciliation and release
v. 13, Personal spiritual warfare

Jesus did not want his disciples to slip into the prayer patterns of the religious leaders of his day, whom he accused of praying for the purpose of being noticed by others. Rather, he desired that they cultivate intimate union with the Father, who would richly give them their proper reward (Acts 1:14).

All ministries of the church need to be bathed in prayer. The early church was born in a prayer meeting. Although Jesus had promised the disciples they would be his witnesses in Jerusalem, Judea, Samaria, and the ends of the earth, he commanded them to first wait in Jerusalem until the Holy Spirit would empower them.

For ten days they waited in prayer and anticipation. This experience of waiting and praying proved exceedingly fruitful, for at the climax of this waiting period 3,000 people turned to the Lord. As the Holy Spirit empowered those 120 disciples, they were anointed for a ministry which turned Jerusalem upside down.

Prayer for Boldness

Ephesians 6:18-20; Colossians 4:2-4

Not only are the disciples of Jesus to pray for new workers and to commission them, they also are to pray for boldness. Paul, writing from his prison cell in Rome, was very much aware that his fear of persecution or even of death might deflect him from an effective and bold witness. Even though he was a seasoned apostle of the Lord by this time, he sensed a timidity which could sabotage an authentic witness for the gospel. For this reason, he asked the church in Ephesus to pray for him.

Praying Together

The late Dr. J. Edwin Orr of Fuller Theological Seminary has done extensive research into the great spiritual awakenings of the past. At a meeting of missiologists in Lancaster, Pennsylvania, in 1984, he said that every great revival in history began with repentance and prayer among Christians. God apparently releases the dynamic power of the Holy Spirit when Christians open themselves up to confession, repentance, and a willingness to be used of God in sharing the gospel.

One of the exciting ways in which modern Christians are working together in prayer ministry is to establish *concerts of prayer.* This term has become well known, particularly through the work of David Bryant, who has lectured widely and written a book to promote the concept. Concerts of prayer often bring together diverse kinds of Christians from different denominations to pray together for the advancement of God's kingdom on earth. God honors such agreement in prayer by releasing his Spirit in unprecedented ways.

The National Prayer Committee of Madison, Wisconsin, outlines helpful ways in which Christians can pray together for the release of God's Spirit in church renewal and expansion. They suggest that Christians concentrate on two major agenda: (1) for Christ's *fullness* to be revealed in his church to empower them for the task which Christ gave and (2) for the *fulfillment* of his saving purposes among the nations through an awakened, committed church.

Many growing modern churches have persons commissioned as prayer elders to lead the congregation in its prayer ministry. Although such a person may have various assignments, the following job description is somewhat descriptive of the duties for a *prayer ministry coordinator*:

1. To maintain a consistent personal prayer ministry.
2. To give serious attention to the study of prayer:
   a. Biblical instruction regarding prayer,
   b. Prayer in classic Christian writings,
   c. Prayer in contemporary writings,
   d. Biographical study of effective prayer warriors.
3. To provide training for persons who desire increased effectiveness in prayer.
4. To coordinate a 24-hour prayer watch in the congregation including
   a. A prayer chain,
   b. Small prayer groups (couplets, triplets, quads),
   c. Special prayer during worship services,
   d. One-hour prayer times around the clock.
5. To distribute monthly prayer guides including intercession for
   a. Leadership in the church,
   b. Special congregational needs/events,
   c. Church outreach ministry,
   d. World evangelization.
6. To coordinate bimonthly days of prayer and fasting.
7. To coordinate a weekly all night prayer meeting.
8. To keep the leadership and congregation updated with prayer news.
   a. In the bulletin,
   b. In the church newsletter.

A church in New Danville in eastern Pennsylvania had experienced little or no growth for many decades. It was a fine country church noted for the gracious character and generous spirit of its members. They tried to evangelize, but with little obvious fruitfulness. So they appointed an evangelism commission. Surprisingly the first action of the commission was to begin a 5:00 to 7:00 a.m. prayer meeting on Tuesday. People on their way to work stopped at the church for prayer.

This congregation has experienced a wonderful surprise. The church has begun to grow. Unchurched community people are coming to Christ and becoming members of the church.

For Review, Study, and Discussion

1. In what different ways does God call persons to follow him? Does a call to conversion differ from a call to make disciples? If so, how?

2. Think of the story of Blasio Kigozi. What do you suppose happened to him during his week of prayer and fasting which prepared him to preach to others?

3. Jesus prayed, then called twelve men to be apostles. He asked these disciples to call for laborers for the harvest. What might this teach us about the relationship between prayer and personnel for mission?

4. Is a person's sense of call enough to assure a congregation that he or she should be commissioned? Are there ways to confirm a call?

5. Review the way in which Jesus commissioned his apostles. How important is it that persons be commissioned for various tasks today? What difference does commissioning make?

Action Challenge

1. Bring together a group dedicated to establishing a concert of prayer in your neighborhood.

2. Discuss with your church leadership the possibility of appointing a prayer ministry coordinator for the congregation—volunteer or paid.

3. Covenant with God to pray daily for the fullness of Christ in the church and fulfillment of God's mission in the world.

4. Obtain and use one of the prayer aids listed at the end of this chapter.

For Further Help

Operation World: Handbook for World Intercession.

Available from Operation Mobilization, 121 Ray Avenue, Hawthorne, NJ 07506.

World Christian Prayer Map. Available from Change the World Ministries, P.O. Box 5838, Mission Hills, CA 91345.

With Concerts of Prayer: Christians Join for Spiritual Awakening and World Evangelization, by David Bryant, Regal Books, Ventura, Calif., 1984. Available from National Prayer Committee, 233 Langdon Street, Madison, WI 53703.

Prayer: Key to Revival, by Paul Y. Cho, Word Books, Waco, Tex., 1984. The amazing story of prayer and renewal in Korea.

Touch the World Through Prayer, by Wesley L. Duewel, Francis Asbury Press, Grand Rapids, Mich., 1986. A practical description of the people of God in prayer ministry.

Chapter 3

The Team

Aurelius Augustine of fifth-century North Africa was converted from a life of self-centered sin and corruption. He became bishop of Hippo and one of the most significant theologians of all time. It was he who helped Christians understand that the word *Trinity* is our inadequate way of trying to say that God is love.

God himself experiences perfect, harmonious, loving communion. Within God there is perfect fellowship and love. Through Christ, through the presence of the Spirit of God around the world, and through the work of creation, we see God's love revealed in fullness and in glory. God desires us to love one another just as he loves within himself. So when we use the word *Trinity*, we mean that God enjoys loving communion within himself, that he has revealed that love to us through Jesus Christ, and that he desires us to love each other as he loves.

The gospel is the gracious intrusion of the precious gift of divine community into human experience. We are invited to love one another and God, just as God loves (John 17:20-26). It is, therefore, no wonder that in the New Testament the missionary enterprise was almost always carried forward by teams. The missionary teams working together in love and harmony were a sign revealing what the nature of the gospel is, the story of reconciling love.

Acts 2:14

Remember, when Peter preached the first Christian sermon he was not alone. He was surrounded by 120 other believers, and as he preached, the other eleven apostles stood with him as he proclaimed the word. We can imagine their "amens" frequently punctuating the air, lending support and credence to what Peter was saying.

Acts 13:1-3

In the book of Acts and in the Gospels, we find that the pattern of team ministry was followed consistently. There were exceptions, such as Philip, who was whisked by the Holy Spirit out into the wilderness, where he shared the gospel with an Ethiopian riding in his chariot. Instances of one-on-one witnessing of this nature are mentioned elsewhere in the New Testament. A good example is Jesus sharing the gospel with Nicodemus alone at home at night. The emphasis on team ministry is not to suggest there is no place for one-on-one witness. We are well aware that in many situations confidentiality and privacy are the most effective means for communicating faith.

Nevertheless, it is also true that when the believers reached out through church planting, the Acts record suggests that the ministry was always carried forward by a team. They apparently never commissioned a missionary to go alone into a new region to plant churches. A noteworthy example is the commissioning of Paul and Barnabas, accompanied by John Mark, as missionaries to the Gentiles. These men were commis-

sioned by the church in Antioch to plant churches among
people who had never heard the gospel.

The Team Is a Church

There are five reasons why a team is essential for church
planting. First, the team in ministry is already a church, even
thought it is a small one. The team working together in
repentance and harmony reveals to people the nature of the
church which it desires to create.

It is not strange that the church at Antioch commissioned a
team, for the leadership there was an interesting group. Two of
the leaders were from Africa, and one of them was apparently a
black man called Niger. Another of the leaders was probably a
Greek and perhaps one or two were Jewish—quite a
heterogeneous team!

The world at that time was seriously divided by racial and
ethnic divisions. The church at Antioch was a new development. This congregation, made up of people from many different racial and ethnic backgrounds, led by persons from three
continents, was unprecedented. This Antioch church was so
unusual that the pagans gave them a nickname: Christians. For
the first time the followers of Jesus were called Christians. The
citizens of Antioch recognized that the love which bound this
church together was the gift of Christ. The multiracial and
multiethnic leadership of this church was a persuasive testimony that God was indeed doing a new thing. They also expected the team of missionaries they commissioned to exemplify the spirit of reconciling love which was present in the Antioch church.

Acts 15:36-41; 16:1-3, 6-7, 11-12

As people see the way team members relate to one another
with loving commitment, they perceive that the gospel which
is being proclaimed is not empty words but reality. The team
may consist of two or more people.

It is sometimes hard to maintain a happy team relationship in mission. The early church experienced some disasters. John Mark left the first missionary enterprise, and this angered Paul. It surely dismayed the Antioch church as well! Later on, Paul and Barnabas had a sharp division of opinion and sadly they separated. Living in a team relationship calls for grace, repentance, and a lot of forgiveness. It demands mutual counsel and accountability.

An Asian church father, Basil of Cappadocia, wrote, "Living alone a man seeks only his own salvation, which is contrary to the law of love. . . . He has no one to correct his faults. . . . God has made us like the delicate parts of the body to need each other's help. . . . Men in community share each other's gifts. . . . How can anyone be humble, merciful, or patient, unless someone else is there? Whose feet will you wash, whom will you serve, how can you be least of all, if you are alone?" (John Foster, *Church History, The First Advance*, p. 151).

The break in the relationship between Paul and Barnabas was tragic. To use Basil's words, they had apparently not yet learned to "wash one another's feet." The fruitful ministry of Barnabas seems to have diminished. Paul returned to Asia Minor where he and Barnabas had teamed together on the first missionary journey. Imagine the dismay of these young churches when they observed that Barnabas was not along with Paul. One can surmise the conversation:

"Paul, praise God, it's wonderful to have you back again! And where is Barnabas?"

"Well, we had a falling out."

"Oh? A falling out?"

It is not surprising that the Holy Spirit forbade Paul from preaching in this region of Asia Minor and that his ministry now shifted to Europe. There is no evidence that Paul ever visited these churches again. Paul's letter to these churches of Galatia shows that they had doubts about his apostolic authority. It seems that his witness among these churches may have been curtailed by the rupture in the team relationships. Paul's ministry was effective when his relationships with his teammates revealed the reconciling grace of God.

Jesus prayed for the unity of his followers, desiring that they be one, just as he and the Father are one (John 17:22-23). This is a sign to unbelievers who are observing Christians.

It is practically a truism to suggest that when a leadership team is divided in spirit or purpose, the congregation will reflect that division. Unity among the team should be of first importance to a pastoral leader. In most situations, any decisions of note must be agreed upon by consensus of the leadership team before the decision is implemented into congregational life. Team meetings are an excellent place to test ideas and receive counsel from one another.

The Team Can Be Diverse

A second reason for a team is that culturally dissimilar persons can help when planting churches cross-culturally. Let us examine Paul's second missionary journey from this perspective. He left Antioch with Silas, with whom Paul shared similar cultural perspectives. Neither of them were Greek, although both had been considerably influenced by Greek culture. Paul had been commissioned to plant churches among the Gentiles, and this would include planting churches in Greek communities.

With this in mind, it is not surprising that at Lystra Paul invited Timothy to join him and Silas, who had taken the place of Barnabas. Timothy's mother was Jewish and his father Greek. Timothy stood between two culture groups, as a cross-cultural person. Often such an individual can be an effective change agent, providing he does nothing which alienates him from the group to which he relates. He stands both within and outside the group which he is attempting to change. This is a helpful stance for influencing change. This team of three traveled to Troas on the western tip of Asia Minor, where Luke, a fourth person, joined them. Luke was a well-trained Greek, a European professional. As an insider, he understood the Greek-European culture thoroughly.

When the team crossed the Bosporus Straits to begin their church planting ministry in Macedonia and Achaia, they were attuned to the challenge at hand. For Luke, the region was home. He understood the culture of the people. There was Timothy, sociologically equipped to be an effective change agent. There were Paul and Silas with their traditional roots in Judaism. In addition, Paul understood people because of his years as a businessman in Asia Minor and his training in theology and philosophy. He was able to incorporate many different styles of leadership into his team ministry.

It was important to Paul to have a cross-cultural team which included persons from the culture in which he intended to create churches. The church planting team commissioned from Antioch included only Paul and Silas. So before he began the new church planting in Macedonia, he invited into the team two additional persons who were not members of his home congregation. As the mission unfolded, the Holy Spirit brought together an expanded team. This team was now equipped for the challenging task of planting the church in a community which was culturally alien from anything Paul had experienced.

In Philippi, the team worked effectively. At the climax of their ministry, Paul and Silas were put in prison because of a confrontation with the exploitative financial institutions of the city. It is likely that Luke and Timothy were exploring various connections they had in the town during the night of the imprisonment. They may have helped to arrange for Paul and Silas's release the next morning. A native to the area, Luke had better connections with the persons in power than did Paul, who was a stranger. It is, therefore, not surprising that the next morning the magistrates dropped the charges against Paul and Silas.

The strength of the team was also evident when Paul and Silas needed to leave Philippi after the crisis. Luke and Timothy remained behind to encourage the church in the aftermath of the anti-Christian riots. In crisis, this diverse team came through with mutual support and strength. It was true as an Eastern proverb says: "One stick can be broken, but a bundle of sticks is too strong to break."

The Team Shares Power

Acts 6:1-7

The third reason team leadership is important is that it provides a way in which power can be shared. When a church planting takes place in a cross-cultural community and the church planting team reflects the variety present in the developing church, authority in the new congregation will be immediately diffused among the various communities. Luke, Timothy, and later Titus the Greek, were significant in helping to establish the churches which Paul planted among the Greeks in Europe. Titus and Timothy became church leaders who helped to demonstrate to those Greek churches that persons of their own culture were qualified and trusted to give leadership to the church.

It is not always possible in the first stages for the church planting team to include all the ethnic communities who will be touched by the new congregation. In that case, the team needs to expand and incorporate new persons into the leadership as the congregation emerges. A precedent for responsibility sharing was seen in the Jerusalem church shortly after Pentecost. The Greek-speaking widows felt their needs were being neglected by the church, so the apostles took decisive action to incorporate into the leadership of the church seven persons who came from the Greek-speaking Jewish community. Those seven persons were commissioned to attend to the needs of these widows. Responsibility was shared, and the Greek-speaking members felt incorporated.

Team Members Assist Each Other

A fourth reason why a team is important is that it brings together a number of laborers who can assist each other in ministry. Especially in the urban context, the size of the evangelistic harvest is overwhelming. How could one person possibly do the job? Interestingly, many persons are named as Paul's co-workers in his urban church planting ventures.

Study the following list of persons who are named as partners in ministry with Paul, either in the Acts or in one of Paul's letters:

Achaicus	Aquila	Aristarchus
Artemas	Barnabas	Carpus
Claudia	Clement	Crescens
Demas	Epaphras	Epaphroditus
Eubulus	Euodia	Fortunatus
Gaius	Hermogenes	Jesus (Justus)
John Mark	Linus	Luke
Onesimus	Onesiphorus	Phygelus
Priscilla (Prisca)	Pudens	Secundus
Silas	Silvanus	Syntyche
Sopater	Sosthenes	Stephanus
Timothy	Titus	Trophimus
Tychicus	Urbanus	

We do not know how large the team was at any given time, but we do get the idea that Paul worked in many team relationships.

The Team Produces Synergy

A fifth reason why a team is important is that synergy is produced by persons who work together. As referred to by pharmacists, the concept of synergy is that the simultaneous action of separate chemicals working together has greater total effect than the individual ingredients.

Gordon MacDonald describes how this phenomenon works with horses. One horse can normally pull about two tons, but two horses working together can sometimes pull as much as 23 tons. That is synergy! (MacDonald, *Restoring Your Spiritual Passion*, pp. 198-199.) This concept seems appropriate in the context of the church, where two persons can often do more than twice the work of one. Interestingly, the word *synergy* is derived from a Greek word, *synerges*. Paul used this word to describe his relationship with Priscilla and Aquila, Urbanus, Timothy, Epaphroditus, Philemon, Mark, Aristarchus, Demas, and Luke. He also used it for others whom he calls "fellow workers." (See Romans 16:3, 9, 21; Philippians 2:25; 4:3; 1 Thessalonians 3:2; Philemon 1, 24.) As persons work together, there is a strength and creativity which cannot be matched by the efforts of persons working alone. The promise of God is that one shall chase a thousand, but two, ten thousand (Deuteronomy 32:30). That is synergy.

We have seen that the apostolic church commissioned church planting teams. We have mentioned five reasons why a team is desirable for church planting.

1) The team working in harmony is a sign of God's love.

2) The cross-cultural team provides special strength when taking the gospel from one culture to another.

3) The team provides a model for sharing authority and responsibility.

4) The team provides for a massing together of the laborers which are needed for bringing in the harvest.

5) The team produces synergy, providing for a greater total effect than working individually.

There are, of course, the additional factors of mutual support and encouragement, as well as accountability.

Let the wisdom of the sage conclude this section: "Two are better than one, because they have a good return for their work: If one falls down, his friend can help him up. . . . Though one may be overpowered, two can defend themselves.

A cord of three strands is not quickly broken" (Ecclesiastes 4:9-10, 12).

Jesus Modeled Team Ministry

Matthew 10:1-4; Mark 6:6b-13; Luke 10:1

Jesus, of course, is the supreme example of kingdom extension through team ministry. At the very beginning of his public ministry he called around him twelve men whom he commissioned to be his apostles. They ministered with Jesus.

Even when he commissioned them to go out and preach the gospel, he never sent them out one by one, but two by two. In the list of Christ's apostles in the Matthew account, they are even named in pairs. They were to travel together and preach together as a team, then return to him to share what had happened. Sometime after Christ had appointed and trained the twelve apostles, he sent out 72° others in pairs. Could it be that each of the six pairs of apostles had each trained six teams of two persons? This would have been quite consistent with Jesus' method of disciple making. In any event, the team model of mission which flows all through the book of Acts was a model which Jesus himself exemplified.

Paul Had a "Prison" Team

2 Timothy 4:9-13

Even when in prison, Paul persisted in Jesus' model of team ministry. He always seemed to have several people around him. Why did Paul want Timothy and John Mark to join him in Rome with the parchments (see his letter to Timothy)? Was Paul hoping to work with John Mark at recording a biography of the Lord Jesus Christ, perhaps the Gospel of Luke itself? What a writing team that must have been in Rome when they were all together: Luke, John Mark, Timothy, and Paul, work-

---

° Some manuscripts indicate 70 here instead of 72.

ing with the parchments which Timothy brought!

Whether on the road or in prison, Paul modeled Jesus' example, working in a team relationship to carry out God's mission.

Spiritual Gifts and Team Ministry

Romans 12:3-8; 1 Corinthians 12:4-11; Ephesians 4:11

One approach to team ministry is to build on the concept of spiritual gifts. Peter Wagner, in his book, *Spiritual Gifts Can Help Your Church Grow*, explains how each spiritual gift can contribute to the growth of the church. In some detail, he illustrates how 27 spiritual gifts which are mentioned in the New Testament relate to the task of church growth. According to Wagner, a person can lead the church to growth with only two spiritual gifts—the gift of leadership, and the gift of faith. Other persons on the team or in the congregation can use their gifts to complement the primary leader's gifts.

Bill Gothard, Katie Fortune, and Keith and Marian Yoder, as well as others, have put special emphasis on the seven gifts which are mentioned in Romans 12:3-8: prophecy, service, teaching, exhortation, giving, leadership, mercy. Some persons feel that every leadership team should have all seven of these gifts in operation in order to have a balanced approach to ministry.

Still others look to Ephesians 4:11 as the definitive word for team ministry. Often *fivefold ministry* is a term used to designate Paul's teaching about apostles, prophets, evangelists, pastors, and teachers. In this sense, apostles and prophets function in a foundational ministry which gets the church off to a good start. Certainly Paul and Barnabas exemplify this ministry. God uses evangelists to draw people into the church, often in large numbers. Philip, in his ministry in Samaria, exemplifies this function. Pastors (shepherds) and teachers build on what has been done by others. These were often persons whom Paul addressed in his letters to the churches.

Significantly, Jesus is the only person in Scripture who bore all of the above titles. Those of us who follow will need to be content to share those functions with others whom God has gifted and called. To think that we could do it alone would be the height of folly.

Other Approaches to Team Ministry

In another approach to team building an experienced person leads the team and a less experienced person assists. This is, of course, a helpful approach to training as well as to team building. As a general rule, it is helpful to have apprentices working with a team. As these persons gain experience, they can be commissioned to lead other teams.

In most of the examples of team ministry given up to this point, no mention has been made of married partners. The church planters were single, or else they functioned without notable mention of a spouse.

Sometimes a married couple see themselves as a team. That is, they believe they function better when they work together at the leadership task, with each performing complementary ministries. Without the contribution of both, there would be an obvious gap in the overall ability to lead. Other couples function with one of the spouses taking a lead role; the other is simply supportive. We believe it is never wise to assign a married person to plant a church unless the spouse shares the vision for the new work. The loving commitment of the spouses to one another and to the work at hand is a necessary sign of the nature of the new church which is being planted.

Each married couple will need to work out ways in which the church planting task can be shared. Paul worked with a husband-wife team that shared the leadership task on a seemingly equal basis. In the references to Aquila or Priscilla, she is sometimes mentioned first, and sometimes he. (See Acts 18:2, 18, 26; Romans 16:3; 1 Corinthians 16:19; 2 Timothy 4:19.) This couple worked together in a beautiful way and God used them to help Apollos, an effective teacher, grow in his ministry.

In most cases, it is probably not advisable for a married couple to work alone in church planting. Another couple or single person will be an asset in helping to get a new work started. While it is true that Christ commissioned his apostles in teams of two, it is also true that they were not married couples. We believe that when married couples are commissioned, they need the support of others in the work of planting a church.

Whatever approach is used to build teams, it is important that the fruit of the Spirit flourish and grow in the team context. This will provide the seed for dynamic church growth.

For Review, Study, and Discussion

1. Think of the reasons why a team concept is important for church leadership. How might this be true especially of church planting?

2. How did the apostles demonstrate the importance of team relationships in the Jerusalem congregation?

3. Reflect on Jesus' sending out his disciples in pairs. Why do you suppose he did this? In what settings might one use this kind of strategy effectively today?

4. Reflect on the disagreement between Paul and Barnabas. How might separation have affected their witness?

5. What is the significance of a cross-cultural team when ministering to people of another culture?

6. Why do you suppose Paul had so many different persons traveling and working with him? How might we use his strategy effectively in itinerant evangelism today?

Action Challenge

1. Think of the leadership team members in the congregation of which you are a part. Try to classify them according to

their spiritual gifts, personality, or temperament. How do these gifts complement each other? How might they create tension in the team?

2. Use a Bible concordance to look up the references for each one of the team members named as partners in the apostle Paul's ministry. Jot down some observations about each of the relationships.

3. Ask for an interview with a church planting team. Try to discover the positive aspects of the team ministry, as well as any negative aspects. How might team relationships be strengthened?

For Further Help

"How to Plant a Church" Seminar, sponsored by Charles E. Fuller Institute of Evangelism and Church Growth, P.O. Box 91990, Pasadena, Calif.

Your Spiritual Gifts Can Help Your Church Grow, by Peter Wagner, Regal Books, 1979. A theological and practical study of gifts used to build up the church and develop ministries which contribute to church growth.

A Theology of Church Leadership, by Lawrence O. Richards and Clyde Hoeldtke, Zondervan Publishing House, Grand Rapids, Mich., 1980. A penetrating study of biblical approaches to servant leadership.

Restoring Your Spiritual Passion, by Gordon MacDonald, Thomas Nelson, New York, 1986. A helpful description of ways to remain joyful, energetic, and fruitful in ministry

Church History, the First Advance, by John Foster, Society for Promoting Christian Knowledge, London, 1972. A well-documented description of the early church, including its spread into Africa, Asia, and Europe.

Team Ministry, by Dick Iverson, Bible Temple Publications, Portland, Oreg., 1984.

Chapter 4

Vision, Plan, and Opportunity

The ancient Huns of the grasslands of Central Asia were a barbaric people, the scourge of the civilized world. These wild nomadic persons seemed to be beyond the missionary capability of the first-century church.

Although missionaries did not venture into the lands of the Huns, the Huns captured quite a few Christians for slaves, during their raids to the south. Some of these Christian slaves told their masters the story of Jesus, and a few Huns became believers. Then in the fifth century, the grandson of one of these captured Christians, Ulfilas, put down the Hunnish language into writing, translated the Bible into the language of his masters, and taught them to read. Ulfilas's ministry was the forerunner of the kind which modern groups, such as Wycliffe Bible Translators, are involved in around the world. By developing a written Hunnish language, Ulfilas made it possible for the slave masters to read of Jesus Christ through the pages of Scripture. Ulfilas used the slave experience as an open door for introducing the gospel. Instead of despairing because of a hopeless and tragic situation, Ulfilas and others in the condition of slavery far from home and friends, used this occasion as an opportunity for the gospel. Thus, through the witness of Christian slaves, the Huns gradually became Christians.

The Holy Spirit Leads

Acts 16:6-15

Creating communities of the kingdom happens as people like Ulfilas see God's vision for the world. Often the first step toward planting a church begins with a general vision of the need to share the gospel with people who do not know Jesus Christ. Then as the congregation and individuals pray, the vision becomes more focused and a particular people or community become the center of the vision. Then specific steps must happen as plans are developed and implemented for the vision to become reality.

Consider the story of the first recorded church planting in Europe. Vision, plan, and opportunity flowed together in the church planting outreach to Philippi. Paul and Silas had left the home church base at Antioch to give encouragement to the new churches of Asia Minor. As they traveled, Paul gave counsel and encouragement to the churches which he and Barnabas had planted on the first missionary journey. After visiting these churches, Paul wanted to go on to preach the gospel in the north, but the Holy Spirit forbade him.

Timothy joined Paul and Silas during their journey through Asia Minor, and finally the rather discouraged trio arrived in Troas on the western tip of Asia Minor. It was here that Luke, a native of Europe, joined the team. It was also in Troas that a vision of a man appeared to Paul, calling, "Come over to Macedonia and help us." We do not know who this man was. Was he an angel? Perhaps Luke himself appeared in Paul's vision. In any event, the call was unmistakable and the team determined that it was the mind of God for them to go to Macedonia to proclaim the gospel.

The Bridgehead

With spirits lifted, they quickly traveled by ship from Troas, crossed the narrow Bosporus Straits, and landed in Macedonia in Europe. The vision now began to form a specific plan. They traveled inland to Philippi, the principal city of the entire region. By planting a church in Philippi the gospel eventually reached the whole area, for cities affect the countryside. A city such as Philippi was the center of political power, economic strength, and cultural vitality where philosophy and religion thrived. A church begun in this kind of place would affect the entire culture.

All church planters need a starting point. This is true both for rural and urban situations. The church planting team in Philippi looked for an opportunity to begin the foundation for the new church. Church planters sometimes refer to this as the bridgehead. Paul frequently used military analogies for interpreting the gospel, and such an analogy seems appropriate here. In military operations, a bridgehead is formed when troops successfully land behind enemy lines and are able to establish a small, defendable foothold which is expanded as more troops join the force. That first foothold is the bridgehead.

Paul and his team found an entry point, a bridgehead into Philippi. In many communities that bridgehead was the Jewish synagogue. These people were near to God, a people of the Scripture, who were anticipating the coming of the Messiah. These Jews were known as the diaspora (the movement of Jews to places such as those mentioned in Acts 2:1-13). Many of these Jews were Greek-speaking and were respected participants in the Gentile community. When groups of Greek-speaking Jews of the diaspora believed in Jesus, they often became a wonderful bridgehead into the Gentile community. From these synagogue communities, the gospel moved outward into other communities, touching the Gentile believers who were in tune with the teaching of the synagogue, although not members of the Jewish community. From the Gentile believers, the gospel began to penetrate the polytheistic, pagan communities which were everywhere.

Apparently, there was no Jewish synagogue in Philippi, so they needed to find another point of entry. On the Sabbath they decided to go to the river, where they hoped to find some people worshiping the Lord. They were not disappointed. Finding a few women there, they joined them in worship. Perhaps this small group of devout women did not seem to be a very promising bridgehead. Yet they received the gospel, and this was the entry point for the gospel into Philippi.

One of the group was a woman of means named Lydia. She invited the evangelistic team into her home for the duration of their stay. Of course, they accepted her hospitality. It helped to establish their presence in the community, and permitted Lydia to express her appreciation for the gift of salvation.

Expansion

The bridgehead was now established in Philippi. The next step was to expand the community of faith for it to take firm root in the Philippian society. The acceptance of the gospel in the home of Lydia and the few women who were worshiping with her is analogous to beginning a house fellowship when a church planter moves into a new community. This core group is a great encouragement, but only the first step in a master plan to reach a whole city with the gospel. That master plan can be fulfilled only as the house fellowship reaches out patiently, faithfully, and vigorously to the surrounding community.

Now that a core group had been formed in Lydia's home, Paul and the team began to expand the witness right into the heart of center city. They went into the marketplace daily to speak with people about the gospel.

The Historical Moment

Progress was rather slow, and they began to experience considerable opposition from a demon-possessed slave girl who could foretell the future. Interestingly, this apparent obstacle to the gospel became, by God's grace and power, the historical moment in which the gospel was able to impact the entire region with significant power. The turnaround came when Paul, through the power of the Holy Spirit, commanded the demon to leave the girl. She was now useless to her slave masters who made much money through her abilities to foretell the future. The cleansing of the slave girl led Paul into a collision with the financial powers of the city. The money men instigated an ugly riot in which Paul and Silas were arrested. The magistrates ordered these two church planters to be beaten and put in prison.

That night an earthquake shook the prison. The jailer was terrified and nearly committed suicide. Paul dissuaded him, and the jailer and his whole household believed in the Lord. The magistrates were embarrassed by what they had done and decided to release Paul and Silas. Paul refused to leave, however, until the magistrates had come and first apologized to him, since it was illegal to imprison a Roman citizen without a trial. Paul had the pleasure of "forgiving" the worried and apologetic magistrates for illegal acts against him.

By the time Paul and Silas had left Philippi, people in the government, the financial structures, the market system, and certainly those poor who identified with the slave girl, had all been confronted with the gospel in an unmistakable way. The confrontation with the slave girl provided an historical moment in which the gospel was able to touch a wide spectrum of Philippian society. That was God's appointment.

Paul and his team needed to be alert to the opportunity which the opposition provided. Had they backed off when they began to experience opposition, the moment would have been lost and the little church in Lydia's home would probably have continued to putter along as a single cell house fellowship for some time. As they reached out in faithfulness, they perceived the implications of the historic moment and used it to the glory of God. By being alert to opportunities at hand and flowing with the mind of the Spirit in a time of frustration, the apostles impacted a whole city for God. In fact, all of the surrounding region was touched by the gospel of our Lord Jesus Christ.

Galatians 4:4

Church planters must be alert to the opportunities for presenting the gospel. The text in Galatians shows God was in tune with the historical moment when he sent the Messiah into the world. He came to earth at the right time and at the right place. He was born in Palestine which is the bridge between continents. He was born during the Pax Romana (a time of relative peace in the Roman Empire), when large areas of the world were ruled by one government. The Greek language was widely spoken. This enabled the gospel to move quickly from people group to people group without crossing the barriers of nation-states. Never has the world experienced such a prolonged period of peaceful stability as it did following the birth of Christ. This period of peace permitted the gospel to extend from China to Spain and from England into sub-Saharan Africa within six centuries.

Jesus came when the world was beginning to seek a universal faith, morality, and community which transcended the petty divisions of provincialism and nationalism. He came when the diaspora had scattered Jews here and there on earth. Everywhere these Jews settled, they spread belief in one God and one morality based upon the Ten Commandments. These scattered Jewish communities introduced Old Testament beliefs and values into many Gentile communities from Spain to India and along the northern tier of Africa. At the time of Jesus there was intense longing for the Messiah throughout the Jewish community, wherever they had settled. (See for example, Luke 2:25-38.)

Indeed, the coming of Christ at that time in history to the Jewish people in Palestine shows that God plans carefully. In a similar manner, every church planter should plan and be alert to the historical moment which God brings into the experience of the newly planted church. We should embrace that moment of opportunity when the gospel speaks to the community with relevance and power. Sometimes it takes many years of faithful ministry until the moment of opportunity becomes clear. The opportunity is not always a crisis. It may be an open door for quiet ministry, or the conversion of a person, that God uses to reveal the glory of the gospel to the whole community.

Obstacles and Stepping-Stones
Acts 8:1-8; 11:19-26

Even persecution and obstacles can become stepping-stones for the gospel. The periodic persecution which the early church experienced in Jerusalem scattered Christians and the gospel to other communities. This is what happened in Antioch when a number of the believers who fled from persecution in Jerusalem preached the gospel to the Greeks. These believers saw, in the midst of tragedy and dislocation, an opportunity to proclaim Jesus to unreached people. Consequently, a new church sprang up in Antioch (Philippians 1:12-14).

One might assume that the imprisonment of leaders would impede the spread of the gospel. Not so! Paul rejoiced that through his imprisonment even the household of Emperor Caesar was touched with the gospel of Christ. The power center of the empire was beginning to be subverted by the Lord Jesus Christ. Thus, Paul was excited about the possibilities for the future of the church.

Furthermore, Paul had time to write while sitting in a prison cell. His letters from prison have been a blessing to the church, and form an essential part of our New Testament today.

Vision and Faith
2 Corinthians 10:14-16; Romans 1:8-15; 15:23-24

Church planting is born from a vision, given by the Holy

Spirit, of God's love for lost people. That vision leads us on to new frontiers of ministry and evangelism. That is how Paul lived. He saw opportunities for church planting everywhere: in regions beyond, in Rome, in Spain. Faith and vision were Paul's greatest resources. Wherever these resources are present, the church experiences growth in ministry and outreach.

Paul earnestly desired to go to Rome to share the gospel. He wrote about this vision in his letter to the Romans, and Luke mentioned it in the book of Acts as well. Rome was the last frontier for the gospel. That city was the center of imperial power. From Rome, the gospel could spread throughout the empire. Paul did not let financial constraints or even imprisonment deflect him from this mission. Yet Rome was not the last frontier for Paul after all. In his concluding paragraphs to the Romans, he astonishes us by announcing that he saw the thriving church in Rome as a stepping-stone, making it possible for him to be commissioned as a missionary to remote Spain.

The vision compels the church planter to move on until all peoples have had the opportunity to respond to the invitation of Jesus Christ. Every faithful congregation, every church planter, every Christian should pray for God's vision to become our vision. Although "Rome" may be the immediate church planting frontier, where, then, is the "Spain" which lies beyond the immediate challenge? Many new congregations devote the entire offering from their first public worship service for mission among an unreached people group. That is a sign that the new church already sees "Spain" in its forward vision.

Every situation presents an opportunity for the gospel. Church planting is always appropriate, because the opportunities and the need are always there. When there are obstacles, those obstacles need to be transformed into stepping-stones for the spread of the gospel. When the doors seem to be wide open, then we march through those doors with thanksgiving. When the doors seem closed, we patiently and persistently pray them open. In every situation, we must pray to be alert to the historical moments God reveals in his own providence so the gospel may be expressed in its fullness and glory.

Obedience to a Vision

Acts 26:12-23

Paul, in defense of his apostolic calling, told King Agrippa about the vision which he saw on the road to Damascus. The vision was so clear that to disregard it would have been disobedience. He testified, "I was not disobedient to the vision from heaven. First to those in Damascus, then to those in Jerusalem and in all Judea, and to the Gentiles also, I preached that they should repent and turn to God and prove their repentance by their deeds." After this vision from God, the Apostle Paul apparently never doubted his call. The risen Christ appeared to Paul in such glory that he could never dismiss the scene from his mind. He spent the rest of his life living in obedience to that vision.

Vision has become a catchword in today's language. It usually means that which is seen by a leader and must be articulated to others. In their book *Leaders: The Strategies for Taking Charge*, Bennis and Nanus say that to be successful in business, vision is essential. A leader must have a clear picture of what is desirable. He must be able to articulate that vision so others can grasp it as well. In this sense, the word *vision* shows what is ahead and uncharted. It is in the future tense.

The biblical picture of vision is different. In every instance, the biblical character spoke of vision in the present or past tense. Paul had a vision on the Damascus road. Peter had a vision on the housetop. John had a vision on the island of Patmos. In each case, the vision had vital implications for the future. But the vision was not a humanly constructed picture of what was to come. The vision came from God as an instruction for action.

Jesus spoke many times of his communication with, and obedience to, the Father. (See John 5:19, 30; 8:28; 12:49;

14:10.) This should serve as an example to any enterprising church planter, who must learn to "see what God is doing" before trying to make things happen.

Growing churches who are reaching out in faithful mission and ministry are characterized by leaders who have a vision from God. The vision usually comes as a result of prayer, fasting, and reading the Word. It is often concerned with renewal or growth. After God has unmistakably shown himself to the church planter or church leader, the vision can be shared with others. Many times the vision is contagious and soon attracts others who believe the vision is from God. In most cases, the scope of the vision is too large for the leader to accomplish alone. In fact, God gives vision to demonstrate that he alone can bring the vision to pass.

Like the apostle Paul, church leaders who have seen a definite vision from God dare not disobey. Often they make sacrifices to obey what they believe God is saying. As recorded in the Scripture, visions were often of brief duration, with little detail. The vision needed to be translated into practical implications for action. The following section explains four ways to translate vision into reality.

Translating Vision into Reality

First, a church planter must have clearly outlined *priorities*. While these may not be on paper, they must be understood in a person's mind. In his little booklet, *Tyranny of the Urgent*, Charles Hummel makes a helpful contrast between the "urgent" and the "important." While there are always seemingly urgent tasks at hand, a church planter must focus on the most important things to accomplish. Not only must the church planter have clearly outlined personal and/or family priorities, he or she must also lead the church in setting priorities.

Priorities are closely aligned with one's approach to ministry, or what is often called a *philosophy of ministry*. Some churches emphasize good preaching. Others emphasize a family atmosphere. Still others consider prayer ministries as most important. Some place emphasis on ministry to specific needs. In the same way, jail ministries, ministries to singles, and ministries to mothers of preschool children are developed. Some churches flourish through the use of a bus ministry. Others bring new people to Christ through evangelistic visitation teams. Still others reach people via radio and television programs.

Different methods reach different people and express an individual approach to ministry. It is helpful for people in a new church planting effort to define carefully their philosophy of ministry and to test whether or not it fits the community in which they intend to minister. For example, it may be unadvisable to begin a day care center in an area occupied largely by retired persons.

One's priorities and philosophy of ministry need to be made specific in *goals* and *plans*. The goals are the specific accomplishments one hopes for. The plans are the specific steps required to accomplish these goals. After goals are set, plans must be laid. In many cases, church leaders find it difficult to make plans specific enough to reach their goals. For every goal, there should be a plan. In other words, one must answer the question: "How do I intend to achieve my goals?"

Pray for each step in the process we have outlined above. However, do not substitute prayer for planning or planning for prayer. God expects us to use the two together.

The Muria Church in Indonesia has grand growth plans. In the mid-1980s their membership in metropolitan Jakarta was a little over 500 in about a half dozen congregations. Their goal is a membership of 10,000 by the year 2000! That goal seems completely unrealistic. Yet the leadership smile as they explain that they are ahead of schedule; they expect to exceed the goal.

The plan to achieve the goal, is simple and achievable. They plan in three-year steps. The plan is easily understandable. It is called the 1-3-1 plan:

—Each person in three years is to lead another person to faith in Christ.

—Each congregation in three years is to plant another congregation.

—Each rural district in three years is to plant an urban church.

To grow from 500 to 10,000 in fifteen years seems unrealistic and impossible. When the grand goal is reduced to three-year planning segments, it becomes not only achievable, but provides each person, congregation, and district with a specific plan of action toward the goal. Posters clearly outlining the three-year plan provide constant reminders of the responsibility each must carry in order for the plan to be fulfilled.

Prayer is foundational to all of this planning and effort. In the mother church at Gudus in Central Java, as many as 100 young people gather for prayer every morning at five, before their day's work or school responsibilities. Prayer permeates the planning, witness, and ministry of the Muria Church. This church frequently experiences considerable opposition. They realize that human effort alone is inadequate. They know they will fail without the empowerment of the Holy Spirit.

For Review, Study, and Discussion

1. What comes to your mind when you think of the word *vision*? What is your definition of the word?

2. Think of two New Testament examples of persons who had a vision. What action followed?

3. How did Philippi fit into Paul's plan for evangelizing Europe? Why did Jesus and Paul emphasize ministry in urban centers?

4. How important is planning in the overall strategy for church planting? How do plans and opportunities relate to each other?

5. How important is the "historical moment" in evangelism? Can you think of biblical examples other than the ones cited in this chapter?

6. Review the relationship between priorities, philosophy of ministry, and goal setting as they influence the planning process. How important are these elements in church planting strategy?

Action Challenge

1. In one sentence, state the vision which God has given you for your life ministry. If you are unable to do this, come before God in prayer until you are able to.

2. Read *Tyranny of the Urgent* by Charles Hummel. Then list five urgent things you have done in the past month and five important things which you need to do in the next month.

3. In very simple terms, state your approach to ministry. Attempt to answer this question: "In what way am I best equipped to meet people's needs through the ministry of the church?"

4. List five personal goals which you intend to achieve within the next six months.

5. Set up a two- or three-step plan for the achievement of each goal.

For Further Help

Writing Your History in Advance, by John Wimber, Vineyard Ministries International, P.O. Box 1359, Placentia, Calif. This six-tape cassette series is a helpful guide to the steps involved in five-year planning.

Tyranny of the Urgent, by Charles Hummel, InterVarsity Press, Downers Grove, Ill. A pamphlet with an effective message: invest time wisely.

Chapter 5

The Power of God

Richard and Lois Landis were pioneer church planters in New Jersey. A family whose lives were touched through the new church needed help. Their adolescent son was frequently awakened at night by mysterious scratching on the wall of his bedroom. He was terrified. Pastor Landis visited the lad's room, and quickly observed that the walls were cluttered with lewd heavy-rock-group pictures. Other lewd pictures of rock 'n' roll groups were hidden in drawers. First they removed and destroyed all these evils. The family confessed and sought cleansing for the evils which had been brought into the room. Then in the name of Jesus, they commanded the evil spirit who scratched the walls at night to leave forever. Peace filled the room and the Holy Spirit came upon that little group gathered with the lad in his bedroom. The evil spirit has never returned.

A gathering of Christians meeting in prayer and worship in Wichita, Kansas, became burdened by the production of weapons for war in a local corporation. Several from the group met with the corporate executive. He wept as they shared their witness. He confessed that he was living with a crisis of conscience and asked them to pray for him.

Because of her witness for justice, a young Christian woman in Argentina was imprisoned and severely tortured by the military regime in that country. She was the daughter of church planting missionaries. After she was freed from prison, she came to the United States and found an opportunity to meet Senate leaders. She told her story. People were so moved by her witness that they initiated policies which eventually contributed to improvement in human rights in Argentina.

The early missionaries among the Zanaki people of Tanzania were accompanied by Jonah Itinni. Jonah was probably the only Zanaki Christian in East Africa at that time. One day Jonah took his machete and went looking for trees to cut into rafters for his new home. He found just the right trees in a grove along a brook in a valley about a mile from their intended home. In Tanzania at that time all land was communally owned, so cutting these trees was quite appropriate, except for one thing. Several women heard the chopping in the grove and came running from their homes nearby to tell Jonah that he must stop because this grove was the home of the spirits. They warned him that if he continued to cut the trees, he would die.

Jonah replied, "Jesus is Lord. Therefore I do not fear the spirits and you don't need to fear them either."

However, they were persistent in their objections. Finally in exasperation he said, "I will go and call the pastor. Then we will return and cut these trees together to prove to you that Jesus is Lord over the spirits. We therefore do not need to fear them."

Jonah hastily walked the mile back up the hill to call the pastor to come to help cut down these trees. What would you do if you were a 25-year-old missionary among a people whom you hardly knew? What would you do if you were implored to become involved in this kind of confrontation by the only Christian who was a native of that culture? The pastor decided he had no alternative except to follow the lead of his African co-worker. Together they went back down the valley and cut down the trees that were needed for the rafters of the house. They did not demolish the grove; they took only the trees that were necessary.

Several weeks later, women dressed in paraphernalia for casting spells and curses came to the area were the church planting team was living. They danced around the premises for quite some time, chanting curses and commanding the spirits to kill those who had so plainly violated the sacred shrine of these spirits. No one died!

Many years later, an old women involved in this incident came to church one Sunday morning and committed her life to Jesus. She gave the reason she had decided to do this. Years before, they had already dug the grave to receive the corpse of the person or persons primarily responsible for helping to destroy the grove. She pointed out that up to that time, whenever such a curse was cast on a person, death was always the consequence. That no one had died was proof to her and many in Zanaki land that Jesus triumphed over the spirits. That is why she had now decided to commit her life to the Lord Jesus Christ who has authority over all the powers.

There were many such examples of power encounters as the gospel began to take root among the Zanaki for the first time. The battle raged at many different levels. On one occasion, a bolt of lightning struck the pulpit in the meetinghouse, causing a fire which consumed the building. That seemed to be a defeat for the people who confessed Jesus as Lord. Not discouraged by this setback, however, the church rallied and rebuilt the facility.

Power Encounter

All around the world, faithful churches are involved in confrontation with evil, sometimes in the form of evil spirits, evil governments, or evil institutions, but most often with people who have given their lives over to evil. The church planter and new congregations experience battles with evil powers. Wherever the gospel is proclaimed and a church is formed, there is a confrontation with the powers which resist the gospel.

Acts 16:16-40

The church planting in Philippi experienced confrontation at many different levels. First there was the confrontation with demons when a slave girl was freed of demonic influence. Then they confronted the commercial interests when the merchants tried to disrupt the advance of the gospel. They were afraid that the believers would destroy their unjust commercial enterprise based upon the enslavement of the girl. The church planters also confronted the criminal justice system. When Paul and Silas were put in prison without a trial, the prison was shaken by an earthquake, their chains fell off, and the door was flung open.

Finally, the gospel resulted in a confrontation with the political powers. When the magistrate sent word that Paul and Silas were to be freed from prison, Paul asked them for a public apology for having beaten and imprisoned him without a trial. The gentle, loving congregation in Lydia's house in Philippi was soon involved in a power confrontation with demons, commercial interests, the criminal justice system, and the political powers. This great city would never be the same again.

Acts 19:1-41

When Paul and his companions arrived in the great metropolitan center of Ephesus, they found a small, rather timid group of about twelve God-fearing men. However, their understanding of the gospel was somewhat limited. They had not yet received the Holy Spirit. They were God-fearers of the baptism preached by John and were not even aware of the

Holy Spirit's presence. When they were told about this precious gift from God, they were eager to receive the Holy Spirit. As Paul laid his hands upon them, they received this gracious gift.

When these twelve men were filled with the Spirit, the stage was set for the tremendous confrontation which took place in Ephesus. Before that time they were just an innocuous Bible study fellowship. They did not have the vision, the courage, or the capability to transform Ephesus in the name of Jesus Christ until they were filled with the Spirit. Without the Holy Spirit, it is impossible to confront the powers.

Of course, our world does a lot of confronting. Labor confronts management, peace marches confront the military, nations confront nations, parents confront children. In all human-empowered confrontations, nothing fundamental ever changes, because all are based on "might makes right." The party who musters the most force wins. The strongest dominates. Mao Tse-tung said it well, "Power comes from the muzzle of the gun." That kind of power confrontation cannot *really* transform anyone.

In dramatic contrast, any confrontation empowered by the Holy Spirit really does transform. This is because the Holy Spirit confronts through love-power rather than force-power. Force never changes the inner spirit of a person, but love does transform the person. That is why the cross is the power of God. God confronts and transforms through the surpassing power of the man on the cross who in his suffering and death cries out, "Father! Forgive them!"

The mighty transforming power of Christ crucified is revealed wherever the Holy Spirit is present.

This is why the presence of the Holy Spirit in the small church in Ephesus enabled the Christians to confront the evil spirits who had gripped their city for centuries. The spiritual forces which were in opposition to the Spirit of Jesus seemed to cluster around the worship and veneration of the goddess Artemis, who was similar to the Roman goddess, Diana. An image of the many-breasted Artemis stood in a massive temple supported with 127 white marble columns in the center of Ephesus. This gleaming white structure was one of the seven wonders of the world. Tens of thousands of pilgrims made their way to Ephesus annually to worship within the precincts of this temple and to receive empowerment from the fertility goddess, Artemis. The worship of this goddess involved sexual activities, so temple prostitutes were always available to aid in worship.

The pilgrims bought shrines of the goddess to take home, anticipating that her benevolence would extend into the family household, blessing the worshipers with children, bountiful crops, and prosperity. The ancient myths declared that Artemis had descended from heaven and was able to bestow upon her devotees the benevolence of heaven itself. Her worship extended throughout Asia Minor.

Closely associated with the veneration of Artemis was the practice of various occult activities and spirit veneration. Ephesus teemed with demons who flocked there to revel in the sin and idolatry of the cult of Artemis. Thus, exorcism of demons was a noteworthy art in Ephesus. All sorts of magical devices had been developed which could be used to bewitch a person or to exorcise the curses which the spirits inflicted on people. The Jewish community had also become involved in these exorcism rites.

It was into this situation of idolatry, prostitution, and demon veneration that a small, Spirit-filled congregation of believers in Jesus began to emerge with power. Spectacular miracles of healing were one of the evidences of the power of the Holy Spirit in this congregation. Casting out demons in the name of Jesus was another evidence.

In this magic-oriented culture, persons quickly assumed there was a magical quality to the name *Jesus*. Seven sons of a Jewish high priest attempted to exorcise a demon simply by using the supposedly magical term *Jesus*. The demon's victim jumped on them crying, "Jesus I know and Paul I know but who are you?" The pretended deliverers ran naked, bleeding, and thoroughly embarrassed from the house of the possessed man.

In this way, Jesus was glorified, for people throughout the city recognized that Christ is in no sense another form of the occult. Rather, he is the triumphant Lord of all the powers. Only those who are committed to him as Lord can participate fully in his triumphal victory.

So phenomenal was the confrontation between Jesus and the powers in Ephesus that the whole financial structure of the city trembled. The blockbuster occurred when former practitioners of the Artemis cult brought their books of secret arts and burned them in a bonfire. The books were valued at what today would be about $2 million. This was no small bonfire and no small event. The city was shaken to its foundation by this bonfire and by the following riot instigated by Demetrius, a silversmith. He apparently envisioned bankruptcy. He thought that if everyone turned to Jesus and forsook the occult and the worship of Artemis, his idol-manufacturing trade would be rendered unnecessary. The offshoot of the riot was that Paul, his companions, and the church were vindicated by the city authorities.

During all these events, neither Paul nor the Christians had ever made derogatory comments concerning the goddess Artemis or her worshipers. It is remarkable that Paul and the church could not be accused of speaking against the false goddess Artemis. This confrontation between the Holy Spirit-filled church and the worldly powers had been going on for two full years. In fact, for two years Paul had taught theology in the hall of Tyranus at the center of town. No witness accused him of speaking against Artemis. The confrontation had moved at another level. The Christians were exalting the lordship of Jesus Christ and Christ, himself, was demonstrating his supremacy over the powers of darkness.

1 Corinthians 2:1-5

We cannot exaggerate the contrast between the power revealed in the cross and worldly power—between Jesus and Artemis. During his three-year stay in Ephesus, Paul wrote to the church in Corinth. In his letter he highlighted the central point of the power encounter between the church and the world. "It is the cross!" he explained. The cross is the power of God. This is to say that when the confrontation is performed through human power, the consequences are disastrous. But in Christ, crucified, the power of evil is broken. Jesus Christ crucified and risen breaks the cycle of violence, exploitation, evil, demonic oppression, and personal sinfulness and guilt.

If the church ministers in suffering redemptive love and confronts powers in the same spirit, victory is at hand. Christ did not destroy simply for the sake of destruction. Thus, we believe that the church's confrontation with the powers should never be for the purpose of tearing down people. The confrontation is always narrowly focused against evil. Its purpose is always for the sake of building, of freeing people. Worldly powers enslave and destroy; the gospel liberates and gives life.

Take note! When Christians confront the powers arrogantly or speak in a derogative manner against demons or false gods, they are not walking in the Spirit of Christ. Being judgmental and arrogant does not exalt Jesus. Christians who act in that manner will discover that the powers may well overcome them, just as it happened to the seven sons of the Jewish high priest, Sceva. A North American urban church planter tells of the time he and his spouse drove past an occult storefront. In a spirit of arrogance and outrage, they commanded the spirits, in the name of Jesus, to leave the storefront. The spirits did leave indeed. But they chased the couple for miles down the highway with the sound of buzzing bees. It was terrifying! Christ-centered power encounter is never overcome by the spirits. Christ's power is not exercised with arrogance, never with flippancy. This does not imply, of course, that Christians are to sit back and say nothing when spiritual matters are at stake.

Acts 8:9-24; 13:5-12

In certain situations, the apostles did not hesitate to give a clear, direct rebuke when the gospel was being compromised or opposed. When Philip preached in Samaria, Simon the sorcerer was amazed by the power displayed in the laying on of the apostles' hands. He offered money to Peter, who promptly confronted him, urging him to repent of his wickedness for thinking that God's power can be sold as a magic secret.

Later, Elymas, the magician, opposed the gospel as preached by Paul to a Roman proconsul. In the power of Christ, Paul rebuked Elymas, who became blind, a powerful sign among the magically inclined Gnostics who perceived Elymas as their sorcerer. This incident was a sign that there is no relationship between magical secret powers and the person of the Lord Jesus Christ. It was also proof that Jesus as Lord breaks the power of the magical.

Spiritual Warfare

Ephesians 6:10-20

Several years after the riot and confrontation in Ephesus, Paul wrote to the church from a Roman prison cell. He must have remembered that confrontation as he wrote, "For our struggle is not against flesh and blood, but against the rulers, against the authorities, against the powers of this dark world and against the spiritual forces of evil in the heavenly realms. Therefore put on the full armor of God, so that when the day of evil comes, you may be able to stand your ground, and after you have done everything, to stand" (Ephesians 6:12-13).

Paul goes on, calling on these Christians to stand firmly with the belt of truth around their waist. They are to wear the breastplate of righteousness, equip their feet with the gospel of

peace, carry the shield of faith, and wear the helmet of salvation. They are to fight with the sword of the Spirit and the
Word of God, and pray in the Spirit on all occasions.

Notice that he concludes this description of the Christian's
battle armor with a call to prayer. Luke does not say much
about the prayer meeting which accompanied these confrontations in Ephesus, but we know Paul well enough to be assured
that he and his companions and the church were involved in a
prayer battle. Further in his letter to the Ephesian church Paul
describes explicitly how they should pray for boldness in faithful witness.

There are several basic principles we should recognize in the
power confrontation between the Holy Spirit and demonic
spiritual powers. M. Scott Peck has developed some of these
principles further in his excellent book, *People of the Lie.*

1. *The Holy Spirit, by himself, does not confront the demonic.* The church cannot confront the demonic alone either.
The Holy Spirit fills the church so the demonic can be
confronted by the church in the name of Jesus Christ through
the power of the Holy Spirit. The Holy Spirit must be incarnated in people committed to Jesus Christ in order for
confrontation with the demonic to be possible and effective.

2. *Spirits and demons are quite ineffective unless they have
become incarnated in people.* It is for this reason that demons
resist exorcism. Once they have left the body of a person, they
are relatively powerless.

3. *Demons usually make their home in persons who are open
to the spiritual dimension of life.* They cluster in areas like
Ephesus, where there was strong worship of the goddess Artemis and where the occult was widely practiced. Spiritually
sensitive people seem to be the most vulnerable to demon-
possession.

4. *Demon-possession is sometimes a symptom of a deeper
problem in a person's life.* For example, bitterness, an unforgiving
spirit, or jealousy may open a person to the revengeful power of

spirits. One must let God deal with the root issues if one wants to experience a full cleansing.

5. *Christians' confrontation with spirits is not analogous to the devices developed by the occult in handling demons.* There is nothing magical about Christians casting out demons. Christians' confrontation with the demonic rests on the fact that Jesus Christ is Lord. Only those who live in joyous, obedient relationship with him have the power and the authority to cast out demons in his name.

6. *Deliverance from demons should never be attempted by a person alone.* It must always be done through prayer and fasting and as a body in Christ moving together with one mind in the confrontation and deliverance.

7. *Not all evil phenomenon is caused by demons.* For example, it is our observation that alcoholism is rarely attributable to demonization. To blame one's anger on a demon may be a form of escapism for a person's own responsibility. It is most important for the praying team to discern carefully whether the person to whom they are ministering is demonized. Perhaps repentance or other forms of healing and ministry are necessary in order to get to the root of the problem in the life of the person needing deliverance.

8. *Demons universally recognize the authority of Jesus.* Not only in Ephesus, but in cultural settings everywhere, when the Christian church confronts the demonized in the name of Jesus, demons demonstrate terror. They know Jesus is Lord. Their power has been broken through his death and resurrection. Our observation is that the spirits hear only Jesus. Other religions and some practitioners of the occult do induce spirits to leave the persons whom they have inhabited. The spirit is entreated and cajoled to leave. But those who confront the spirits in the name of Jesus have the authority to command. Our observation is that spirits confronted with the authority of Jesus tremble and obey.

9. *One must enter all such spiritual confrontation with*

prayer and fasting and the humility of authority and boldness which come through knowing Jesus Christ as Lord and Savior.

Luke 19:28-48

Not all power encounters are explicitly related to the demonic. It is true that both the Scriptures and our experience in spiritual warfare demonstrate repeatedly that there is a war raging between the army of heaven and the host led by Satan. The influence of these unseen powers is very real. We battle in prayer and in the confidence that the victory belongs to Jesus. Nevertheless, it is not just Satan and his host who have rebelled against the Lord; humanity has also turned against God. The power confrontation between Christ and the demonic which rages in the heavens also extends into our communities through the occult, the worship of false deities, and various forms of spiritual bondage. The power struggle also confronts us through ordinary human beings who are not demonized at all.

Jesus frequently confronted the demonic and cast out demons with authority and power. He also confronted persons who were not demonized. One of the most astonishing descriptions of such a confrontation is described in each of the Gospels—namely, the cleansing of the temple. The Jewish temple was the center of colossal power. Eighteen thousand Levites served full-time to maintain the temple and its worship rituals. In fact, during the time of Jesus, the temple was undergoing reconstruction. This project employed another 18,000 people. Huge sums of money poured into the temple coffers from the religious taxes which were sanctioned by the Jewish religion. As if that were not enough, merchants contracted a profitable business from within the temple courts. They sold animals for sacrifice to pilgrims who had come a great distance, and took advantage of these pilgrims by overcharging. The courts had become a bedlam of financial racketeering at the expense of faithful worshipers. Instead of being a symbol of ministry, the temple had become a sign of exploitation.

Jesus confronted the merchants with a demonstration of authority so unbearable to the Jewish establishment that they deemed it necessary to arrest and crucify him. He overturned the tables of the money changers, sending their precious cash rolling across the temple pavement in jumbled disarray. Taking a switch, he chased the cattle from the temple area. He shouted to the merchants to be gone. They had turned the house of God into a den of thieves.

Power encounter! Had Jesus functioned only as a gentle teacher with a quiet ministry of healing the sick, he may never have been crucified. It was this confrontation with the authorities which led him to the courts and to Golgotha. It was his confession that he had the authority to act in this way, that he is indeed "the Christ, the Son of the Blessed One" (Mark 14:61), which sealed the verdict that he must be crucified!

Authentic Christ-centered church planting is confrontational, not only with the host of the spiritual forces, but also with people who control the centers of power. When people use those powers to the detriment of the poor or the exclusion of people from opportunity and justice, they are serving evil. Power encounters in church planting often require confronting those who exploit the poor and obstruct human rights. When we love the poor as Jesus loved them, we discover that the task of evangelism also includes the obligation of confronting those who trample the powerless, the poor, and the oppressed.

Revelation 5:1-14

In the book of Revelation, we see a vision of the Lamb (who is Jesus Christ) crucified and victorious. In his confrontation with evil, Jesus suffered. In the same way, the church experiences suffering as we confront evil. But in the suffering there is victory. There is new life. There is a rebuilding of the good. Jesus, the victorious one, destroys his enemies with the weapon of truth. It is the sword that goes from his mouth which overcomes evil. The weapons of Christian warfare are not of human origin. Instead, the weapons are salvation, faith, witness, truth, the Word of God, prayer, and righteousness, wielded by the Spirit of God. These weapons guarantee the victory.

One of the remarkable stories of the church confronting the powers took place in the middle of the nineteenth century when the antislavery movement emerged in England. During the early part of the nineteenth century there was a great spiritual awakening in England, an awakening which also significantly affected the United States. In England, the evangelical fervor was also expressed in a commitment to confront and transform power structures which exploit the poor and enslave African people.

Wilberforce was one of the principal leaders in this movement of confrontation and transformation. As a politician, he organized groups all across England who worked for the freeing of slaves in all countries ruled by England. This movement was permeated with prayer. Wilberforce confessed that frequently he invested three hours a day in prayer for the end of slavery. Prayer permeated his planning and careful organization. In time, the transformation came. Slavery was declared illegal throughout the entire British Empire and eventually throughout the world.

The confrontation against the slave trade and the exploitative policies of nineteenth-century industrial England assured that England would be spared the scourge of communism. Had the church not sought in revival, prayer, and confrontation to transform the evil structures of British society, England would most likely have become a Marxist state. The Holy Spirit empowered the revived church in England to address the evil of the day through prayer, witness, and confrontation in such a way that society experienced a profound transformation. The church wielded the sword of truth with effective power.

It reminds one of Philippi and Ephesus in Paul's day.

Binding and Loosing

Luke 13:10-17; Matthew 12:22-29; Luke 11:14-22

The power encounters described in the book of Acts are simply a continuation of Christ's ministry while on earth. For example, Luke describes the healing of a crippled woman who Jesus said had been bound by a spirit. In a declaration and demonstration of God's power, Jesus freed her from Satan's crippling hold. This act of healing was a visual lesson of God's desire that all of Abraham's children should be free from the power of Satan. It was this kind of ministry which prompted Peter's witness to the household of Cornelius: "You know what has happened throughout Judea, beginning in Galilee after the baptism that John preached . . . how God anointed Jesus of Nazareth with the Holy Spirit and power, and how he went around doing good and healing all who were under the power of the devil, because God was with him" (Acts 10:37-38).

On another occasion, Jesus healed a demonized man who was blind and mute. The Pharisees accused him of using Satan's power to do his work. In response to their accusation, Jesus declared that it was the Spirit of God within him who drove out the demons. Using an illustration about a strong man whose house was pillaged, Jesus implied that Satan's house was being robbed whenever people were freed from demons. But in order for people to be set free from his evil grasp, Satan would need to be bound.

Jesus has already bound Satan's power, and he has graciously given that same authority to the church. This may be one dimension of what Jesus meant when he told Peter and the other disciples at Caesarea Philippi: "I will give you the keys of the kingdom of heaven; whatever you bind on earth will be bound in heaven, and whatever you loose on earth will be loosed in heaven" (Matthew 16:19). The binding power of Satan is broken when the kingdom of God comes, and people are loosed by the Spirit of God. What an incredible power is at the disposal of those who live under the lordship of Christ!

Signs and Wonders

Acts 2:43; 4:30; 5:12; 8:13; 14:3

If one were to cut out all the references in the book of Acts about the extraordinary power of God, only a few tattered fragments would remain. One of the ways in which the writer of Acts draws attention to the power of God is by reference to signs and wonders. As God's kingdom was declared, the people were often astonished to see God's power demonstrated in extraordinary ways. Jesus gave sight to the blind, healed the lame, freed the demonized, and raised the dead. It is in conjunction with these incidents in Acts that we see bursts of growth in the church, whether in the home church at Jerusalem, in the neighboring country of Samaria, or in the distant lands reached by apostolic teams. As one studies the ministry of the apostles, it becomes apparent that they expected God to move in power whenever the gospel was preached. Their expectations were founded on their experiences with Jesus.

Throughout his time on earth, Jesus ministered both in word and deed. As he preached repentance and forgiveness of sins, he demonstrated the power of God to bring healing and restoration. His miracles demonstrated of God's love and reinforced his preaching and teaching ministry (John 20:30-31).

Throughout his Gospel, John draws attention to both the words and deeds of Jesus, emphasizing the importance of belief in Jesus Christ as the Son of God. As depicted by John, the miraculous signs which Jesus performed were for the purpose of prompting belief. Even as the religious leaders tried to discredit Jesus, the people asked, "When the Christ comes, will he do more miraculous signs than this man?" (John 7:31). Because the Pharisees and chief priests scoffed at the works of Jesus, he warned of impending judgment on those who rejected the power of God as demonstrated in miraculous signs. After the healing of the man born blind, Jesus declared: "For judgment I have come into this world, so that the blind will see and those who see will become blind" (John 9:39). Those who witness God's power cannot remain neutral. They must respond in belief, or face God's judgment (Acts 3:1-10; 4:1-22, 30).

On one occasion, Peter and John, met a man at the temple doors who was lame. They healed him in the name of the Lord Jesus Christ. The rulers of the temple, dismayed by this healing in the name of Jesus, whom they had only recently crucified, threw Peter and John into prison. In the trial which followed, they were astonished at the boldness of these uneducated fishermen. When the powerful men in the Jewish nation commanded in court that Peter and John must no longer witness in the name of Jesus, the reply of the uneducated fishermen was, "We must obey God rather than man." Later, in a prayer meeting in which they asked the Lord to give them boldness, the house shook with power from God!

Matthew 7:15-23; 24:23-24

Not everyone who uses the name of Jesus is truly a servant of God. There are some false prophets who prophesy in Jesus' name, perform signs and wonders, and drive out demons, but are under the judgment of God. Jesus warns against these false prophets who try to gather followers by a demonstration of power.

The test of a true prophet is the fruit of Christian character; a false prophet produces rotten fruit. Signs and wonders alone are not enough to prove the validity of one's ministry. People are too easily taken in by the spectacular.

Joy in Adversity

God is sovereign! He does not always lead or act through obvious miracles in the same manner we desire. David Watson describes this kind of disappointment in his spiritual autobiography of death, *Fear No Evil*. Watson, a world-traveled evangelist, contracted cancer in midlife. He and his ministry team believed God would perform signs and wonders by healing Watson miraculously. But God did not heal. Why? Watson's book describes his pilgrimage into death. In the concluding pages written only days before death, he affirms that he believes miracles of healing need to be viewed modestly, only as signs of the resurrection, the guarantee that we all someday will rise again. He asks: If we were all healed, would we really yearn for the resurrection?

The ability to suffer and even die in faith, hope, and joy is also a significant revelation of God's grace. Church planter John Miller contracted brain cancer and entered a large Philadelphia hospital. The church prayed for his healing, yet he died, stricken in the prime of his ministry. In the corridors of that sprawling, impersonal hospital, John's quiet witness of joy, peace, and confidence in Christ became a mighty sign of God's grace and power. Even the community in which he served as a church planter was "exceedingly amazed" by the mighty power of the gospel revealed in this man's death and the gentle, gracious witness of his family during and after this experience. One of the testimonies of the truth of the Christian way is the gift of God's grace, which enables persons like David Watson or John Miller to die with faith, hope and joy.

The precious stories of the deaths of servants of the Lord remind us of the miracle of salvation. When a person hears the call of the Holy Spirit, repents, and is converted, that is the miracle of supreme significance.

Sixteen-year-old Chuck Bordy was sipping a strawberry milk shake with his pastor, at Elby's Restaurant, when he accepted Christ. He was anointed with waves of joy. Chuckling he asked, "Does the Bible really say that angels sing when a sinner repents?"

"Yes!" the pastor affirmed.

"I have no difficulty believing that!" exclaimed this dear lad who had known much sadness. With joy, caressing his face he continued, "Why, I am so happy I can hardly drink my milk shake!"

True servants of God humbly minister in Jesus' name. They expect God to stretch out his hand to perform his own work in his own way and in his own time, including the miracle of converting people. When ministers of Christ begin to step ahead of God in order to establish their own credibility or bolster their own image, there can only be disappointment and judgment. Faith is the ability to trust God and submit to God in all circumstances. It is the ability to marvel at the surprises of God as revealed in both the miracle of healing or the grace of accepting suffering and death with joy and peace. Of course, the greatest sign and wonder of all is the miracle of conversion and new birth.

Christian Compassion

Christian compassion is also a significant "sign of wonder" of the power of the gospel. Around the world faithful Christians express the compassion of Christ with sacrifice and joy. Homes for unwed teenage mothers, orphan care, hospitals, leprosy care, homes for the retarded, famine relief, industrial and agricultural development, urban housing, drug and alcohol rehabilitation ministries, literacy, ministry to prostitutes, care for AIDS victims, psychiatric care—these are a few examples.

Mother Teresa from Calcutta, India, was interviewed on Yugoslavia state television after she was awarded the Nobel Peace Prize for her ministry for abandoned orphans. Yugoslavia is her native country.

"Why do you do it?" her interviewer asked.

With a gentle, joyous smile, she astonished her audience with her reply, "Because Jesus loves me!"

Compassion expressed with sacrifice and joy is a surprising sign of the reality of the gospel.

The implications for church planting are clear. As God empowers there will be significant and fruitful ministry. Even as the apostles preached with a strong conviction in the name of Jesus, so we must declare his kingdom today. And as we see our efforts multiplied and blessed by the Spirit of God, we can address the Father with even greater fervency: "For yours is the kingdom, the power, and the glory, forever and ever. Amen."

For Review, Study, and Discussion

1. Do you agree that power encounter takes place whenever the good news of Jesus Christ is preached? Why or why not? Give biblical support for your answer.

2. Reflect on the relationship between Paul's experience in Ephesus and his exhortation in Ephesians 6:10-20. How does this passage relate to power encounter today?

3. How does the suffering and death of Jesus Christ relate to the battle in which Christians are engaged?

4. Review the suggestions which are given for dealing with the demonic. Do you agree with these suggestions? What further suggestions do you have?

5. What is the relationship between the spiritual forces of evil and an unjust human government? In what ways is the church involved in the struggle between these powers today?

Action Challenge

1. Interview a church planter. Ask about spiritual warfare and power encounter. What insights does this person have about the relationship of church planting and spiritual warfare?

2. Using a Bible concordance, identify several incidents in the ministry of Jesus where he dealt with evil spirits. What might we learn from Christ's experience in this area?

3. Again using a concordance, identify several similar incidents in the book of Acts. What were the evangelistic results of these spiritual confrontations?

4. Page through a current newspaper or magazine. What spiritual activities might lie behind the news stories?

5. What are the evils in your society or community which the faithful church confronts?

For Further Help

Bothered? Bewildered? Bewitched? by Grayson Ensign and Edward Howe, Recovery Publications, Cincinnati, 1984. This book gives practical guidelines to help Christians deal with the demonic.

Power Evangelism, by John Wimber, Harper and Row, New York, 1986. A booklet which studies the New Testament teachings on the role of the miraculous in evangelism, with ample modern examples.

The Presence of the Kingdom, by Jacques Ellul, Seabury Press, New York, 1967. A penetrating theological study of the kingdom of God in the Bible and the indications of the kingdom in modern society.

The Original Revolution, by John Howard Yoder, Herald Press, Scottdale, Pa., 1972. A study of the nature of the life and ministry of Jesus.

Fear No Evil, by David Watson, Harold Shaw, 1985. The spiritual autobiography of Watson as he faced death, even though many had prayed in faith for his healing.

People of the Lie, by M. Scott Peck, Simon and Schuster, New York, 1983. The study of evil from a psychiatric and biblical perspective.

Chapter 6

Developing the Congregation

Mahatma Gandhi drew from many sources in his quest for spirituality. There is no doubt that he was affected by the New Testament, and particularly by the life and teaching of Jesus. A primary reason why Gandhi resisted ever becoming a member of the Christian church is that he believed Christianity had betrayed Jesus. On one occasion he tried to worship in a white church in South Africa, but he was rudely turned away. He desired to lead Hindus into a more dedicated commitment to the teachings of Jesus than was true of Christendom. He was especially impressed with Jesus' attitudes toward enemies and his use of nonviolent resistance in confronting evil, as in the cleansing of the temple. Gandhi worked vigorously at transforming the caste system in India so the social structure of Hindu culture would conform more fully to Jesus' attitudes toward the poor and the oppressed. He was a champion of the disadvantaged.

Sadly, Gandhi never experienced the full implications of the good news of Jesus. No community gathered around him which was explicitly committed to the lordship of Jesus. Some of his ideals were eventually embedded into the laws of India, most notably the prohibition of discrimination on the basis of caste. Nevertheless, no community was formed which could further develop these ideals and become a conscience within Hindu society. Gandhi's vision of nonviolence is now largely lost to Hindus. No church formed with a commitment to living that way.

Habitat for Humanity is a marvelous ministry which creates low-cost housing for the poor. This vision began when Millard and Linda Fuller shared in the commitment for racial and community justice with the Koinonia community which Clarence Jordan had founded in Americus, Georgia, during the height of the civil rights movement. In the mid-1970s, the Fullers began a modest effort to provide housing for the dispossessed in Americus. That effort ignited a fire of compassion. Today Habitat for Humanity helps provide low-cost housing for poor families in scores of cities in America and overseas.

The team of volunteers in Americus has grown. However, few churches in Americus are really committed to the idea. The Fullers and many of the volunteers wish that local, indigenous churches would provide more spiritual support, counsel, prayer, and vision for the ministry. It is not surprising that demanding caring ministries of this nature eventually often lose momentum unless they are nurtured by a local church. A community of faith is needed which is larger than only the volunteers. In Jesus' name, such a church could commission and encourage the ministry. Service efforts and political reform movements eventually run out of energy if they are not sustained by the energizing power of Christ and the church.

Visible Church

Acts 2:41-47; 5:1-11

We are thankful for the work of Gandhi and the sacrificial service for the poor by Christian service volunteers in many parts of the world. However, the New Testament vision is for an explicit and intentional commitment to Jesus Christ. We believe that the Holy Spirit desires to form a church in every community on earth which carries on the vision of Jesus Christ as Lord from generation to generation. It is normal for a congregation of believers to emerge when the gospel is expressed in word and deed.

Jesus said that his disciples are in the world but not of the world. Jesus seems to have perceived his disciples as becoming an identifiable, visible *community* of witnesses within the wider society. Christianized reform movements or service ministries are good, but they are incomplete until these efforts are sustained through the spiritual vitality of local congregations. These local churches become the sustaining energizers for evangelism, cultural or political reform, reconciliation, justice, and service in the community.

That is exactly what happened at Pentecost when the church was first formed. Although the disciples may have hoped that the whole Jewish nation would become believers in Christ, it did not happen. Rather, people were called from the Jewish nation to form the church. This new community was a visible, identifiable fellowship of believers in Jesus Christ as Lord and Savior. This new community was "salt and light" within the larger society.

The first congregations were house churches which met in small clusters throughout the Jerusalem metropolitan area. Since most of the homes in the Jerusalem area were small, we may assume that from ten to twenty people gathered in each of these cell group fellowships. Probably 100-200 of these small congregations, meeting in living rooms throughout the Jerusalem area, were formed within days of Pentecost. Yet they never functioned independently of each other. These home cell groups formed the clusters comprising the church in Jerusalem, a congregation who for some time met around the temple area for celebration events.

Characteristics of the Apostolic Church

The apostolic leaders of the church helped to form the doctrine and lifestyle of those congregations quickly. It may well be that each apostle took responsibility for a cluster of these cell groups—ten or twenty for each apostle. We read that they went from house to house ministering to these congregations that were being formed. These apostolic leaders had been with Jesus and had personally witnessed the Pentecost event. They recognized Peter as their leader, so there was a commonality in their vision. The various cell groups partook of the same experience in community and commitment. They also seem to have united occasionally all together in joyous celebration assemblies. Nine characteristics of this church in Jerusalem are mentioned in the accounts of Acts.

1. *They met together daily.* Regular times of fellowship and sharing were central to the early church. Writing nearly two centuries later, Tertullian in North Africa explained that all Christians must meet for worship and fellowship at least once weekly, even if such assembly meant death. It was essential that the believers gather together regularly..

2. *They were instructed in the apostolic doctrine.* These men who had been with Jesus for three years taught the new believers of Jesus. We can be confident that they drew heavily from Old Testament prophecy and analogy to communicate the faith to these new congregations. Although it was written some time later, the book of Hebrews probably represents the doctrinal tone of the apostolic teaching among these Jewish Christians in the Jerusalem area.

3. *These new believers enjoyed a deep experience of fellowship with one another.* The barriers between men and women which had divided Jewish worship were apparently abolished. A new community, a vibrant fellowship, was being created through the work of the Holy Spirit in their midst.

4. *They loved each other and shared their goods with one another.* No one was left to be without food or shelter or

clothing. In fact, some sold their properties and distributed the profit so all would benefit from the wealth of the participants in the congregation.

5. *They broke bread with each other.* This suggests that they often had fellowship meals together and that these new believers practiced hospitality. They also shared in communion with each other as Jesus did on the night he was betrayed. Reverently, they broke bread and shared with one another in remembrance of the body of Christ that had been broken on the cross for their salvation. They shared the cup of wine together in remembrance of the precious blood of Jesus which was shed for the forgiveness of sins. The breaking of bread was a constant reminder that the heart of the new community is Jesus Christ, crucified and risen.

6. *They shared in prayer with each other.* Prayer permeated the church. Much of the prayer exalted Jesus Christ, but believers also interceded that God would give them boldness to witness fearlessly. When Peter and John were in prison, a group gathered together to pray for them. The Lord intervened miraculously. He sent an angel to free Peter from prison. In prayer, they experienced the power of God through fresh anointings of the Holy Spirit.

7. *The church was anointed with love and joy.* Joy is the touchstone of authentic Christian fellowship which helps to undergird the congregation in times of suffering and crisis. Joy is exceedingly precious, for there is not much of it to be found in any society. But in the group who has met Jesus, joy abounds and so does love—the free, overflowing commitment to minister to one another and to the world in which we live.

8. *These cell groups were centers of witness and evangelism.* We read that the church grew and multiplied exceedingly as neighbor told neighbor the news of Jesus Christ. We may assume that as the little living rooms became packed with people, the groups divided and new cells were formed. Soon the original 100 or so congregations multiplied and became

hundreds of small-group fellowships throughout the whole metropolitan area. They witnessed with power and persuasiveness to the saving acts of God in Jesus Christ. From the descriptions of the witness given by Peter and Paul, we may assume that they also invited a belief in Jesus Christ with urgency. They persuaded people to believe in him.

9. *These congregations practiced discipline.* Ananias and Sapphira sold their land but gave only a portion of it to the church. Because they pretended that they had contributed the full amount to the congregation, the Spirit of God acted decisively. The couple died because they defied the Holy Spirit by acting and speaking untruthfully. This dramatic incident demonstrates the disciplined lifestyle of these Jerusalem congregations.

The Influence of the Church Planter

The previous nine characteristics of the Jerusalem church actually represent an extension of the vision and commitment of the apostles, who were in this case the church planters. Even today, a congregation usually develops a vision and commitment which is quite similar to that of the person or persons who planted the congregation. Just as Peter and the apostles left their enduring imprint on the congregations in Jerusalem, so every church planter or church planting team tremendously affects the form of the congregation. If the planter is charismatic, the congregation will be a charismatic church. If the planter is committed to developing a thriving, viable relationship with the sponsoring denomination, the congregation will echo the same commitments. If the planter has an independent spirit, the congregation will become independent. The new congregation will be formed in the image of the church planter or the church planting team.

It is therefore exceedingly important that every church planter be unreservedly committed to Jesus Christ as Savior and Lord. We have many opportunities to interview potential planters. One of the first questions we ask is: "What is your relationship with Jesus Christ?" We are not interested in planting social clubs, but rather in planting communities of redeemed people who love the Lord Jesus Christ. Although the style of the congregation will vary with the style and personality of the church planter, it is imperative that every new congregation be a fellowship which gathers in the name of Jesus.

It is wise for the planter occasionally to invite other speakers in to minister in the emerging congregation. This is one way in which the congregation can avoid becoming fixated on one person's personality. It is also important to include the ministry gifts of all the team members in the formation of the church. The new congregation must also share in community-wide interchurch events and avail itself of denominational nurture opportunities. The wise church planter consciously helps the new church avoid the extreme influence of the personality of one person.

The Church Planter: A Farmer and a Builder

1 Corinthians 3:1-17

In Paul's letter to the Corinthian church, he explains the role of the church planter in the developing congregation. Essentially, he uses two analogies from everyday experience. The first is that of a farmer, or gardener. Comparing the Corinthian church to a field (v. 9), Paul thought of himself as one who planted the seed. After the seed sprouted and began to grow, Apollos watered it. In either event, Paul asserts, it was God who made it grow. It is, of course, from this passage of Scripture that the term "church planting" derives.

Then Paul takes a slightly different perspective. He compares the Corinthian people to a building (v. 9). The foundation for the building, of course, is already laid, "For no one can lay any foundation other than the one already laid, which is Jesus Christ." The church planter (or church *builder*, to switch to the new analogy) must take care in building upon this foundation. Even as modern architects and builders await the inspection and approval of government officials, so a church builder's work will undergo inspection and testing by the Master Builder. Poor workmanship and the use of cheap materials will result in severe loss at the day of judgment. The building does not belong to the construction workers; it is God's temple. For this reason, it is important to recognize the sacredness of God's investment in people as his dwelling place. One cannot destroy God's building without suffering severe loss in return. What could be more rewarding than the knowledge that one is participating with God in the erection of a temple in which God himself dwells, with "living stones" mortared together by God's grace? (1 Peter 2:5).

There may be yet another lesson in Paul's two analogies to church growth and development. Farming and building are two essentially different kinds of activity. They require different knowledge and skills. A farmer, works with living things. How can one know ahead of time the results of working with plants? In the only parable recorded by all three synoptic Gospel writers, Jesus compared the preaching of God's Word to a farmer who was planting seeds. Some of the seeds were snatched away by birds, some quickly sprouted but later withered in the sun, and some were choked out by weeds.

But the farmer did not despair. Some seeds sprouted, grew, and produced a crop. In a sense, the farmer simply cooperates with God without fretting unduly about the many things that can go wrong. In the same way, the church planter will exert much effort with many people. Some effort seems wasted. But thanks to God who gives the growth, there is also fruit. Jesus reminded his disciples that they were reaping where others had sown (John 4:37-38). In Corinth, Paul did the planting, and it was Apollos who watered. Both were cooperating with God.

In contrast to the farmer, the builder works with more predictable materials. In most cases, careful planning is done and blueprints are drawn before construction begins. The larger and more sophisticated the desired building, the greater is the need for careful forethought of structure and procedure. Careful consideration is given to the most suitable building materials. Most likely, a schedule of activities is posted so that each step of construction follows in proper sequence. The lesson for church builders is clear. Careful planning is essential! As explained in chapter four, Paul had a plan which he followed as he traveled from place to place.

In church development, it is quite helpful to have a plan which outlines the steps for growth. Each stage of growth in a congregation requires adjustment to changing needs. In his book, *Looking in the Mirror*, Lyle Schaller discusses the differing needs of various sizes of congregations and ways in which leaders must adapt in order to be effective. For persons who are by nature nonplanners, the concept of church building by careful planning may seem threatening. However, it is generally true that the larger a congregation grows, the greater will be the need for organization and planning. Within most congregations there are those who can do careful planning. The wise pastor or church builder will identify and call out these gifts as God leads.

Furthermore, the way in which a church begins has a vital influence on the ongoing life of the fellowship. For example, if the church begins as a supper fellowship for persons who have similar cultural or ethnic roots, it may well remain as a group with cultural distinctiveness. Again, if the church begins with a ministry to a specific group of people, or to meet a specific set of needs, it is likely that this will remain the central focus. Or, if small-group development is central to a core group's philosophy of ministry, this emphasis will most likely be seen in the developing congregation. Of course, strategies can change. But tradition, community image, and people's expectations can soon lock an emerging fellowship into a pattern of ministry which is less than effective. The wise builder will not let the principle behind Paul's illustrations be lost to the church today.

Paul and the Corinthian Church

Recent research helps us to appreciate the amazing development of the church in Corinth. Two books which include excellent research on the Corinthian situation are *The First Urban Christians*, by Wayne Meeks, and *The Social Setting of Pauline Christianity*, by Gerd Theissen. These two works demonstrate the complexity and polarization of Corinthian social structures. It is now evident that the Corinthian church wove together the fabric of a new community which united into one new community persons who came from diverse and polarized communities within Corinth. There was no precedent anywhere for what was happening in Corinth. How could this miracle be achieved? It could happen only through building the new community on the foundation of Jesus Christ, alone. That was Paul's mission!

Nevertheless, Paul could not accomplish the mission alone. If it had been just Paul proclaiming that Jesus is the only foundation, most Corinthians would have assumed that he was a misguided fanatic. He planted the seed, then other teachers came along to help water that seed—to cultivate and nurture. Paul planted and Apollos, the articulate teacher, watered. Apparently, even Peter contributed to the discipling of this church. Various leadership gifts helped to form this church. Thus it was against formidable sociological and cultural obstacles that these leaders together in their respective ministries helped to form a new community in Corinth, based on a covenant relationship with Jesus Christ.

The church in Corinth developed in a completely different culture than the church in Jerusalem. Many of the Christians in Corinth had no biblical heritage. They had never heard of the Torah. The culture was thoroughly infused with polytheism. Christian ethics were almost incomprehensible to this society which was noted throughout the Mediterranean region for its evil living. Yet, even in this setting, a church was formed.

Paul began in the synagogue, a community somewhat akin to the Jerusalem community. These people had the Old Testament and their moral values were in close harmony with those of the church. Thus, the synagogue formed a point of entry for the church. Soon persecution developed. It first developed within the synagogue itself, but later the Gentile community also became hostile to the church. The persecution helped to define the new community in contrast to the wider Jewish and Gentile society. House churches emerged, some of which were most likely Jewish (such as the congregation which met in the house of Jason). Others were most likely Gentile (such as the one which met in the home of Gaius).

Opposition as an Asset

Persecution often helps a church define its life and ministry. The Kimbanguist Church in Zaire, Central Africa, suffered greatly under the Belgian colonial government. Simon Kimbangu, the prophet and founder of this church, had a public ministry of only two months before he was forced into hiding for fear of arrest and imprisonment. Yet during those two months of public ministry he emphasized the ministry of Jesus as the reconciler between races, as the one who loves enemies, and as the Healer. Those themes are prominent within the Kimbanguist church even today, some three generations since its founding. Two months of brief ministry, followed by enormous suffering and persecution, helped that church develop its sense of identity and mission—a mission which persists to the present day. In this case, persecution also helped the church grow. Today the Kimbanguist Church in Zaire is probably the most effective community of national unity within the entire nation.

Roger Williams planted the first Baptist church in North America. He arrived in the Massachusetts Bay Colony in 1631 only eleven years after the Pilgrims landed. He believed strongly in religious freedom, which the theocracy in Massachusetts did not provide. Persecution drove him from the colony, forcing him and his followers to form a new community on a tract of land which they called Providence. The persecution which these Baptists experienced in Massachusetts gave the new congregation a firm resolve for religious freedom and separation of church and state. Their experience of persecution helped to define their faith. No wonder the constitution of Rhode Island, where the Baptists settled, guaranteed religious liberty and separation of church and state. A century and a half later this constitution became the model for the national constitution. To this day, Baptists across the land are champions of religious liberty.

Discipling the Church

In Corinth, the persecution helped to define the nature of the church. Yet this was only one factor. Paul invested one and one-half years in a teaching ministry in Corinth. He discipled the new community. First Corinthians 3:11 is clearly the central theme of his discipline: "For no one can lay any foundation other than the one already laid, which is Jesus Christ." This was an astonishing commitment against the backdrop of polytheistic Corinthian society. Certainly most Corinthians could understand the notion that Jesus is a lord, but to insist that he is the *only* foundation was a radical departure from the sectarianism and universalism of the Achaian peninsula. All through his teaching ministry, Paul was forming a covenant community based exclusively on Jesus Christ.

2 Corinthians 7:8-16

It was not easy to be part of the church in Corinth. The world was always attempting to squeeze this new creation into its mold by seducing it away from Jesus Christ. After planting the church in Corinth, Paul's next major church planting endeavor took place in Ephesus, where he ministered for at least two years. Ephesus lies across the Aegean Sea from Corinth, making return visits to Corinth conveniently possible. Apparently Paul frequently hosted guests in Ephesus from the church in Corinth. Presumably, they asked Paul's counsel concerning matters pertaining to life in their church.

Occasionally Paul sent one or more of his trusted colleagues to visit the church in Corinth to give counsel and to encourage them in the way of Christ. On at least three occasions he wrote letters. Two of these letters are included in the New Testament. One of these, known as 1 Corinthians, rebukes the church sharply for inclinations to depart from Jesus Christ. Four major issues are highlighted: (1) polarization in the church based on social class or theological diversity, (2) sexual immorality and improprieties, (3) cultic worship expressions, and (4) compromises in relationship to polytheistic practices. The only defense that Paul perceives against these pressures is Jesus Christ crucified. He reminds the church that Jesus is, indeed, its only foundation.

After Paul wrote this letter, he waited anxiously for many days to hear a response from Titus (the one who was to report). He was apparently fearful that the Corinthian church might have rejected his rebuke. At the same time, he was well aware that he and the Corinthian church were in this matter together. If they rejected his rebuke, it would mean that together they had failed to establish the church in Corinth on solid rock. It was not as though the apostolic church planter was rebuking the Corinthian church with no sense of his own accountability to the church to which he was speaking. Paul was so worried about the Corinthian situation that he was unable to evangelize effectively. Instead, he went looking for Titus, anxious to hear about the state of affairs in Corinth. When he met Titus, he received a good report. Paul was overjoyed. (See 2 Corinthians 2:12-13 and 7:13.) He expressed his joy in another letter to Corinth.

Paul saw his rebuke as an opportunity for the congregation

to define again its relationship to the world and to Christ. In 2 Corinthians 7:12, Paul points out that his letters of instructions are a test which gave the congregation the opportunity to face the choice anew. The issues to which he was referring had to do with sexual immoralities. The choice was between allegiance to Jesus Christ in partnership with the new covenant community, or to become absorbed into the world's system. In this case, the church excommunicated from membership someone who was living with his father's wife. (See 1 Corinthians 5:1-13.) Apparently this person was influential in the community, for the excommunication seemed to have potential for repercussions within the church and the wider community. Yet the congregation took a stand. This witnessed anew to their commitment to Jesus Christ in his fullness.

Imagine the joy of the congregation and Paul when the one who was excommunicated repented of his sins, returned to Jesus Christ, put away the illicit relationship, and was reinstated as a full brother in the Lord (Matthew 18:15-20).

When a fellowship, whether small or large, meets in Jesus' name, that fellowship has the authority to exercise discipline. The church in fellowship with its Lord begins to define lifestyle in the context of the community in which it lives and ministers.

For example, many congregations living in areas where alcoholism is a problem have taken a clear stand: No social drinking is permitted by any member of this congregation! That kind of stand sharpens the witness of the new fellowship as it confronts evil in its neighborhood. Different congregations will be led to draw the boundaries in different ways, but every fellowship needs to set about the business of defining the boundaries of church membership.

Defining the Boundaries of the Fellowship

Paul Hiebert, anthropologist at the Fuller School of World Mission in Pasadena, California, speaks of various ways of defining the boundaries. He explains four approaches:

1. *The bounded set* develops a discipline which clearly defines the line between the world and the congregation. Those who violate the boundary can be excommunicated. People need to subscribe to the boundaries to become part of the fellowship.

2. *The fuzzy set* leaves much room for ambivalence. These congregations thrive on lack of clarity. When a doctrinal or practical issue is raised, the congregation typically decides on the issue by recognizing that "on the one hand there are *these* viewpoints, on the other hand there are those viewpoints among us. Who can really say what is right or wrong?"

3. *The open set* has no boundaries at all. This is typical of a society in which there is a state church system. Everyone born into that society is baptized as an infant and is assumed to be part of the church.

4. *The centered set* recognizes the direction in which a person is facing. If one is facing toward Jesus Christ as Lord and Savior, he or she is then introduced into the fellowship, even though in some practices one may be far from the ideal. The important thing is that the person is moving in the right direction. It may be that someone who appears to be close to the center in terms of lifestyle is actually far from Christ because he or she is moving in a direction opposed to Christ.

The church planter will have a large impact on the stance which the future congregation will take in relationship to these respective approaches to discipline. Whichever approach one takes, it is urgent that the church planter be a person who loves the Lord Jesus and exalts him in personal life and ministry. Church life is authentic only where Jesus Christ is exalted.

The formation of a church is never complete. It is always in progress. The church planter, the leadership team, and the congregation, in partnership and fellowship together, are called by God to be constantly involved in the process of becoming the new creation which God is forming in any society in which a church is present.

For Review, Study, and Discussion

1. Review the nine characteristics of the church in Jerusalem. Can you think of other characteristics not mentioned in this chapter?

2. Consider the idea that a new congregation will always reflect the image of the church planter. Do you agree or disagree with this concept? What are the implications for selection of planters?

3. How did Paul's deep conviction about the lordship of Jesus Christ affect his approach to the church at Corinth? How does Christ's lordship determine our strategy for witness in our communities today?

4. Reflect on the practice of church discipline as modeled by Paul and the Corinthian church. How might this example benefit us in the church today?

5. Review the story of Simon Kimbangu's ministry in West Africa and Roger Williams' ministry in North America. What do these examples teach us about the proper response to persecution?

6. Review Hiebert's four ways of defining boundaries in the church. Which of these reflects your congregation? In your mind, which is the most helpful way?

Action Challenge

1. Share Hiebert's insights about boundaries with your pastor or other church leaders. Using those definitions, how would Hiebert classify your congregation's approach to church membership?

2. Make a list of your congregation's activities and body life together. How does this list compare with the list of activities for the Jerusalem church?

3. Look at your congregation's constitution, covenant, or statement of faith and doctrine. How is the issue of discipline addressed in this document?

For Further Help

Paul's Idea of Community, by Robert Banks, William B. Eerdmans Publishing Company, Grand Rapids, 1980. This book, subtitled "The Early House Churches in Their Historical Setting," is a helpful exposition of the apostle Paul's theology and approach to ministry in the church.

Looking in the Mirror: Self-Appraisal in the Local Church, by Lyle Schaller, Abingdon Press, Nashville, 1984. A presentation of approaches to the self-analysis of local congregations.

Chapter 7

Gospel
and Culture

On the east coast of the United States, Atlantic City is known as the gambling capital. Casinos outline the skyline. Millions of visitors come every year to squander their wealth at the slot machines or the high-stakes gambling tables. Sadness and brokenness characterize the city. The original inhabitants are being displaced as the casinos, with their massive economic power, shove helpless people off the island the city occupies. Prostitution, drugs, and alcohol are an obvious scourge. The gods of pleasure and glittering wealth are worshiped in this place.

It is to this modern-day Corinth that Charles and Donna Arnold were called by God to plant a church. In the summer of 1985, they and their two children moved to Atlantic City. A year before, Charles had resigned his job as a telephone lineman to receive training in a Bible institute in preparation for planting a church in this city.

As with the apostle Paul, it took some time until the Arnolds began to discover effective entry points into the city. Their first house fellowship did not meet in a synagogue as in Corinth, or with women at prayer by a river as in Philippi, but in a small living room with about a half-dozen persons present. Two of them were cocktail waitresses. One of these women was distressed because her teenage daughter had recently been abducted by evil men to make pornographic films. The other was devastated because her teenage son was a demented drug addict. These broken people reaching out for help, among others, comprised the first house fellowship.

Planting a church in Atlantic City confronts us profoundly with the nature of the gospel as it relates to culture. Should the cocktail waitresses resign their $50,000 a year jobs when they become Christians? No other jobs seem to be available in the Atlantic City area. Should the bus driver who shuttles persons to the casinos resign his job when he becomes a Christian? These are not silly questions. They get at the heart of what it means to be a church in a modern-day Corinth. How does the gospel confront culture redemptively? How does the gospel redeem people caught in the web of an evil culture?

Dealing with Cultural Issues

Acts 15:1-35

The apostolic church struggled with the same kinds of issues. An interesting description of a church conference working through the issue of gospel and culture is described in Acts 15. This conference is also referred to in the first and second chapters of Galatians, where Paul describes the events from his perspective.

Clusters of cell groups were forming among the Jewish people in Jerusalem. Several years later, another cluster of house churches developed in the Syrian metropolis of Antioch, 300 miles north of Jerusalem. Mostly Gentiles comprised these Antioch congregations who soon commissioned missionaries to take the gospel to other Gentiles. Paul and Barnabas (and later Paul and Silas) carried the good news of Jesus Christ far to the west. In a short time, many thriving Gentile churches were planted in significant metropolitan centers within Asia Minor. Before long, these missionaries from Antioch preached in faraway Europe and perhaps they also shared in mission to India.

The Jewish congregations in Jerusalem and these new Gentile churches were culturally quite different. Jerusalem and Antioch were only 300 miles apart, but the cultural distance between these two urban centers was enormous. European Corinth and Jerusalem were utterly alien to one another from a cultural perspective. Note some of the contrasts between the Gentile culture of Corinth and the Jewish culture of Jerusalem.

Jerusalem

1. Knowledge of the Old Testament.
2. Old Testament biblical ethics.
3. Belief in one Creator God.
4. Belief that God calls out a covenant community which is open to anyone.
5. Religion, diet, and ritual based on the Old Testament.
6. Intense longing for the coming of the Messiah.
7. Belief that nature is good, but it is not divine, and that it is to be used for the good of humankind.
8. Belief that history has meaning.
9. Strong family life.
10. Belief that all males in God's covenant community must be circumcised.
11. Convinced that they are God's special people, a light to the nations.

Corinth

1. Almost no knowledge of the Old Testament.
2. Moral chaos accepted as the norm.
3. Belief in many gods.
4. All human community based on tribe, social status, or occupation.
5. Religion, diet, and ritual based on polytheism or tribal practices.
6. No awareness of any Messiah who is to come.
7. Belief that nature is evil or at least not as good as spiritual realities, and that it is chaotic and divinized.
8. Belief that history is meaningless.
9. Unstable family life.
10. Abhorrence of any defacement of the body, including circumcision.
11. No sense of mission beyond personal success or the success of one's particular group.

Throughout the centuries a few Gentiles had become Jewish by becoming absorbed into the Jewish or Old Testament cultural milieu. In the same manner, the Jerusalem church believed that all Gentiles who believed in Christ should become circumcised. By the time the church was beginning its missionary expansion, there were already many Gentiles who believed in God as revealed in the Old Testament. They appreciated the morally uplifting teachings of Judaism, but were unwilling to submit to Jewish diet, dress, and ritual practices, including the rite of circumcision. So these God-fearers stood on the periphery of Judaism longing for more inclusion, while remaining outsiders.

When the church was formed, many of these Gentile God-fearers eagerly embraced the Christian faith because in the church they found a spiritual home. However, many of the Jewish Christians still thought of these new Gentile believers as outsiders. "You must be circumcised in order to become full members of the covenant community, the church," insisted these Jewish believers. They pressed this demand for the Gentile believers even though circumcision was abhorrent to them. Thus the stage was set for a major collision between Gentile and Jewish Christians.

The crisis sharpened in Antioch, the first thriving Gentile Christian community. This church was growing rapidly. Some scholars believe this church soon included 500,000 Christians. It was a missionary church, sending persons like Paul, Barnabas, and others north into Central Asia and east into Mesopotamia and Persia. The Antioch church was involved in helping to plant the thriving congregations of Edessa in Mesopotamia, who became exceedingly dynamic in missionary outreach for the east. Soon the Antioch church would share in translating the Bible into their own Syriac language.

Nevertheless, the nagging question from the Jewish perspective was whether the Antioch church was really part of the covenant community. Could they really be the people of God when they had not submitted to the clear teaching of the Old Testament as regards circumcision and dietary practices? Some of the Jewish brethren from the church in Jerusalem visited the church in Antioch to attempt to encourage the believers there to become circumcised. Tremendous confusion ensued. These people had experienced the transforming grace of our Lord Jesus Christ. Their lives had been changed.

Early church leaders such as Bardaisan of Edessa in Mesopotamia or Justin of Samaria describe the moral transformation expressed by the Christians (John P. Kealey and David W. Shenk, *The Early Church and Africa,* 1975, pp. 185-186). These and other descriptions show us that broken homes were healed, drunkards were rehabilitated, and thieves no longer stole. Idolaters put away their idols, those who practiced magic renounced their sorcery, husbands stopped beating their wives, incest ceased, violence was renounced, peace replaced vengeance, and love for one's enemy replaced hate. The change in people's lives was clearly visible.

The power of the Holy Spirit had been released in this community. Joy and love filled the congregations. The fruit of the Holy Spirit was revealed in the lives of the Christians. So noteworthy were these new phenomena in Antioch that the onlooking pagans nicknamed this new community "Christian." Apparently this came about because the Christians conducted themselves in a Christlike manner.

Wisely, the leaders in Antioch decided to take specific steps to resolve the crisis. Their approach to this issue is helpful to churches everywhere who struggle with similar questions. Whenever new congregations are planted, similar issues arise. The manner in which the church in Antioch and Jerusalem approached the problem is relevant for today.

What did they do?

1. They sent a representative delegation from the church in Antioch to Jerusalem to meet with the apostles and elders.

2. They discussed the issue openly. They swept nothing

under the carpet. They all recognized that the question before them involved not only the problem of cultural differences, but also the question of biblical interpretation or hermeneutics.

3. After clarifying the issues, they listened to reports from the apostles and missionaries concerning what God was doing among the Gentiles. First Peter spoke. He reminded the group of the miraculous way in which God led him to share the gospel with Cornelius and his family—a Gentile household. He reminded them of the marvelous way in which the Holy Spirit was revealed in that home.

Then Paul and Barnabas began to tell of the work of the Holy Spirit among the Gentiles of Asia Minor. The assembly was silent as Paul and Barnabas told of the miracles of God's grace on the island of Cyprus, in Antioch of Asia Minor, Iconium, Lystra, and Derbe.

4. They examined the Scriptures in light of the fresh outpouring of the Holy Spirit upon the Gentile people. They discovered that this movement of the Holy Spirit was in harmony with the vision of the prophets of old. The fresh outpouring of the Holy Spirit enabled them to discover treasures and truth within the Scriptures which they had not been aware of before.

5. In prayer, discussion, and listening to the Holy Spirit, and with the Scriptures before them, they came to a decision by consensus. With boldness and confidence they accepted the authority which Jesus himself had given to the church. In chapter five we observed that one dimension of the church's authority to bind and to loose may refer to the binding of the power of Satan and the loosing of his power on a person. At the Jerusalem conference we see another dimension of the church's authority to bind and to loose (Matthew 16:19). Although in this circumstance, the loosing of the requirement for circumcision meant a wrenching reinterpretation of traditional understandings for many of the Jewish leaders, they nevertheless experienced confidence that their decision was guided by the Spirit. At the same time they also bound certain practices. For

example, they prohibited the eating of the meat from strangled animals. The church confidently both "bound" and "loosed."

6. They wrote a letter which openly recorded the decision of the church. They knew that this letter would become a lightning rod for attack by self-styled leaders who had not been present at the conference. Yet they were committed to being people of the light. They desired that the truth of their decision be fully revealed. The nature of this decision was so controversial that it was imperative for the action of the council to be stated in language clear and understandable to all.

7. They sent the letter to the churches by the hand of a representative delegation. This group was responsible for answering questions and communicating the spirit and the intention of the conference. Both a letter and an official delegation were commissioned to interpret the decision.

Resolving Issues Today

The five dimensions of the decision process are noteworthy. They form a blueprint of how the church in mission should work at resolving issues related to the gospel and culture. Not only is the blueprint of the decision process important, but also the principles involved in the decision are significant. What are those principles?

1. Flow with the movement of the Holy Spirit.

2. Test your perception of the movement of the Holy Spirit with the Scripture and the counsel of the whole church. Be aware that we can fall into the trap of being too subjective. The story of God's acts in history as revealed in the Bible are foundational to understanding whether the movement is from the Holy Spirit or from another spirit.

3. Recognize that practices involving ritual or symbolism are culturally relative. A practice such as circumcision, for example, may be meaningful to Semitic people, but repugnant to Japanese. Cultural practices having to do with diet, ritual, or amenities should usually be seen as significant only within the

local cultural context and not perceived of as universal values. For example, the holy kiss of New Testament times (1 Corinthians 16:20 and other references) may suggest homosexuality in many modern cultures. Therefore, that symbol of brotherly love may not be applied universally.

Each Christian community needs to think through the use of ritual, symbols, and practices which truly express the meaning of the gospel in the respective cultures. In this case, although the Gentile churches were freed from the symbol of circumcision, they were required to express their separation from idolatry by abstaining from meat offered to idols *and* from the meat of strangled animals. Although ritual and symbolism are culturally relative, they are important.

4. Recognize and embrace universal commitments which are transcultural. For example, the moral commitments of the Ten Commandments are universal. The Bible does not condone moral relativity. Thus, even in a culture which celebrates deception, truthfulness needs to be the Christian stance. Even in a culture which celebrates theft and dishonest gains, followers of Jesus will attempt to be honest in all their dealings.

The Jerusalem conference freed the Gentiles from bondage to Jewish cultural practices, but at the same time called them to submit to the universal moral and spiritual commitments of the Christian faith.

The examples which they highlighted had to do with practices related to the worship of false gods and premarital sexual intercourse. These were common practices within the Gentile communities where the churches were being planted. The new family of God was called to repent of these false and evil practices.

5. Work toward the goal of preserving the unity of the church. The manner in which the consultation took place was in itself an attempt to preserve church unity. Also, the decisions revealed a concern for harmony.

Adjusting to New Circumstances

Romans 14:1-23; 1 Corinthians 8:1-13

You will recall that one of the decisions which came out of the Jerusalem council (Acts 15) commanded that Gentiles abstain from eating meat which had been offered to idols. Some time later, this command became a problem to the church in Corinth. They apparently wrote to Paul asking for his counsel. His response is recorded in the passage from the Corinthian letter noted above. The issue which faced these Corinthian believers concerned polytheistic practices. Apparently all the meat sold in the public market of Corinth was sanctified by the idols before it was available for public purchase. This fact presented the Christians with two problems. On the one hand, if they ate meat offered to idols, it might bring division into the church, for many Christians would perceive this as a compromise with idolatry. On the other hand, to abstain from buying meat at the public markets meant that Christians either must become vegetarians or that they should open their own "Christian meat markets." The issue revolved around the desire to maintain unity and a clear witness, while trying to be sensitive to practical issues.

Interestingly, Paul did not tell them what to do. However, he freed them from the specific requirement of the Jerusalem conference that they should not eat meat offered to idols under any circumstances. He indicated that in this circumstance, it might be appropriate for them to buy meat from the public market. They should decide on the matter, keeping two considerations in mind. First, they must be clear in their witness that they did not venerate false gods. Second, they needed to be concerned about preserving the unity of the church and avoid offending weak brothers and sisters.

Here we see that Paul (with his apostolic responsibilities) and the congregation in Corinth decided together to "loose" something which had been "bound" by the Jerusalem conference. But note, there was no loosing of the undergirding concern of the Jerusalem conference to maintain clarity of witness and the unity of the church. On those issues there could be no compromise.

Unity with Diversity

The decisions of the Jerusalem conference freed the church to experience unity with diversity. No other community on earth enjoys so much exhilarating cultural diversity. At the same time, Christians everywhere who are committed to Jesus Christ as Lord experience the mystery of unity in Christ. How can it be that the church, now present in all nations on earth, continues to experience this special kind of unity?

Cultural anthropologists and sociologists help us understand some of the dynamics involved in these phenomena by comparing cultural practices to an onion. There is an inner cultural core which is the worldview. The worldview is the way in which a people within a culture understand the way the world is. It is their perspective on the cosmos. The worldview sets the tone for the entire culture.

Surrounding that central core are layers of cultural expressions. These layers may be likened to the skins of an onion. The first layer is the values or mores of a culture. This is the level at which we make decisions about right and wrong.

The second layer of our cultural onion is comprised of practices. This is the manner in which people conduct themselves. It is what they do with their time and the kinds of social organizations they develop.

A third layer is artifacts. These are the things a culture makes: the houses people build, the clothing they wear, or the means of transportation they create.

There are other layers to our onion as well, but these four dimensions of culture are significant summaries of all that goes into making a culture.

Let us illustrate how this works. A central perception of Americans is described in the Declaration of Independence. All persons are "endowed by their creator with certain inalienable rights." Among these are "life, liberty, and the pursuit of happiness." Individualism and protection of human rights are of high value in this worldview. Many laws have been developed both within the framework of the American Constitution and outside of it to protect the rights of the individual. For example, police can not enter the home of a suspected criminal without a warrant based on significant evidence.

Many other practices reveal this commitment to individualism. For example, rather than develop an adequate means of public transportation for the towns and suburbs of America, Americans build highways at enormous expense on the assumption that persons will use their own individual cars to go to work. Artifacts which affirm the individualistic orientation abound in American culture. Another example: most family residences have multiple bedrooms—one for each child—not to mention an automobile for each member who drives. Thus, our culture expresses an individualistic world view in its artifacts.

How does the gospel relate to all of this? That is exactly the question of the Jerusalem conference. How does the gospel interact with these various layers of culture? Many people in the early church perceived that the point of interaction between Jesus Christ and a culture is primarily at the practice and artifact level. They were concerned about the kind of clothing people wore, what they ate, and the signs of Christian commitment such as circumcision. These were primarily demonstrations at the practice and artifact levels.

Modern-day anthropologists have demonstrated that the artifact and practice levels of a culture are the areas where change comes most easily. However, change at that level is the least significant for creating a shift in personhood. It is at the worldview core and the level of values that change needs to take place if it is to be genuinely creative in the culture or in the persons participating in the culture.

It is at the deep levels of worldview and values that Jesus spoke with the most power and relevance. And that is exactly what the church affirmed. They decided to address the issues of the Christian faith from the perspective of belief and values. They decided to be more relaxed concerning the outworking of those beliefs and values in the realms of practice and artifacts.

Dynamic Equivalence

Principles used in modern Bible translations help us understand how a congregation should relate to its cultural milieu. Eugene Nida and others have developed the concept of "dynamically equivalent translations" (Eugene Nida and Charles Taber, *The Theory and Practice of Translation*, 1969, pp. 3-8). These linguists argue that translations of the Bible should not strive to replicate a literal word for word rendition of the original Greek or Hebrew text. Rather, the creative translator attempts to understand the meaning of the text to the original audience, and then to communicate the same meaning for the modern audience. For example, it might be that a dynamic equivalent translation of "I am the true vine" for a modern city dweller would be "I am the true electric socket."

Congregations need to express their lifestyle in a manner which is dynamically equivalent to New Testament faith and practice. Congregations in Muslim countries may decide to worship on Friday instead of Sunday. In some West African societies it may be that the minister should sit rather than stand to preach. The communion bread in Zaire may be made of yams instead of flour. The faithful church in mission always seeks to express New Testament faith and practice in forms which communicate dynamically with the contemporary culture.

Christ and Culture

Richard Niebuhr outlines five different ways in which the church has responded to the question of Christ and culture.

They are as follows:

(1) *Christ against culture.* Christ is understood to be against all cultural expressions. Persons who have these perceptions withdraw into sects with their own expressions of faith.

(2) *Christ of culture.* Churches tend uncritically to embrace their cultural surroundings. There is an impressive similarity between the church and the surrounding culture. This approach stands in strong contrast with number one above.

(3) *Christ above culture.* The church is the primary determinant of cultural expression in the world.

(4) *Christ and culture in paradox.* Some groups perceive church and culture to be two separate, but related movements. The church lives its own life, without much influence on the surrounding culture.

(5) *Christ, the transformer of culture.* This approach assumes that the church must make a difference in the world by functioning as a positive influence. To us, this seems to be the way Jesus anticipated for his followers. He told them they were salt and light to the world (Matthew 5:13-16).

Luke 6:1-11

Frequently during his ministry, tension developed between Jesus and the guardians of practice. A significant tension point had to do with Jesus' approach to the Sabbath. The biblical scholars of the day were impressed by the rigid application of the Sabbath which was practiced by their forebears. These practices had roots deep in the Old Testament tradition. In fact, there had been a time when people were put to death for violating the Sabbath for even so minute an offense as picking up sticks for cooking supper.

In contrast to these rigid persons, Jesus healed a crippled person on the Sabbath. He also permitted his disciples to pluck grain to relieve their hunger as they walked along the roadway. The keepers of the law were furious and terribly offended. They even plotted to kill Jesus. However, Jesus attempted to help them understand that the "Sabbath was made for man, not man for the Sabbath" (Mark 2:27).

That statement was a worldview blockbuster. The keepers of the law believed that they needed to keep the Sabbath in order to please God. By submitting to this law, no matter how inconvenient, they would earn merit and the approval of God. Jesus attempted to explode this perception. Contrary to the viewpoint of the keepers of the law, Jesus revealed that the Sabbath is a precious gift from God to humankind. It is an invitation to experience rest on a regular, weekly basis. The Sabbath is God's gift of grace to humankind which we are invited to receive with joy.

Thus we see that Jesus was primarily concerned about touching the worldview and values of people. He knew that if we are touched at that level, the practice and artifact levels of culture will find their appropriate places. It is in that same spirit that the apostolic church worked with decisions related to the interaction between the gospel and culture. Of course, both Jesus and the early church were aware that these issues touch the bedrock question of biblical interpretation. Throughout the Old Testament and even in the New Testament, we are occasionally given specific guidelines concerning practice and artifacts. And the question with which we struggle in biblical interpretation is to what extent those kinds of directives should enjoy universal application. We do not attempt to lay to rest all of those kinds of questions. They are very real and very significant.

However, it is important to understand that both for Jesus and the apostolic church the greatest concern was that the good news of the kingdom be received into the core of the believer's life and values—into the center-point of interaction with the culture. When that happens, the question of whether it is right to eat meat offered to idols or not to eat such meat can be viewed with the sensitivity of spirit which comes through the experience of Christ living within.

This is to say that there must be consistency with the Holy Spirit, the worldview, the value, the practice, and the artifact levels of our being. Often, however, a new congregation developing within a particular cultural framework sets about determining what practices and artifacts are acceptable and which are not acceptable to the new Christian community. Once that is determined, then the church considers that it has now become established with clearly defined differences between the new faith community and the world in which it lives. There is the danger that these definitions at the artifact and practice level may become substitutes for the inner reality of the gospel. Instead of the believers permitting the Holy Spirit to form them into the image of Christ, they begin to focus on issues.

Consider, for example, the actual case of a congregation which experienced a marvelous revival. As the Holy Spirit worked within the fellowship, they became more and more persuaded that Christians should rely only on the protection of the guardian angels of God, and not on any protective devices designed by humans. They lived in a high crime area. Soon the church was split over the issues of whether it was right or wrong to have watchdogs. The "nonwatchdoggers" separated from the "watchdoggers." The watchdog had become a symbol disproportionate in its significance to the more important quality of Christian experience—love for one another.

That is what was happening in the Galatian church when Paul wrote his letter to them. This beautiful congregation was concerned that they might miss the highest good which God had for them, so they attempted to define their faith through rituals and customs. They began to set aside sacred days and attempted to act religious. These Gentiles even considered circumcision. They felt this would help them become better Christians. After all, circumcision would be a sign to the whole world that they had really cut their ties with all the evil in Gentile culture.

Paul was deeply dismayed by this tendency on the part of the Galatians to substitute form for faith. So he wrote a letter encouraging them to remember that they are justified by faith in Christ, not by customs. He asserted that it is the ongoing life of Christ within the believer who shares in the worshiping, discipling community of believers which is the essence of the new creation. The essence of new life can never be captured fully through customs or rituals.

Nevertheless, custom and ritual are important, for they become symbols which help to communicate the faith. For example, baptism and communion are practiced by most Christians around the world. These symbols help to communicate the meaning of the gospel. The need for new birth, the need to receive Christ daily as our food and nourishment, or the need for forgiveness of sins are communicated through these symbols. Thus, they are important. But if in the practice of these symbols we do not meet Jesus, then we have really missed the point of having them.

That is the burden of Paul's letter to the Galatians.

And what about Atlantic City? That congregation will need to counsel with the wider church as they attempt to find the way of our Lord Jesus Christ for them in that community. The central questions in all their considerations should be: What is Jesus Christ doing in Atlantic City through his Holy Spirit? What guidance do we get from the Scriptures? What is the counsel of the wider church? In this manner we will find the way together in the churches which have been planted in our modern-day Corinths.

For Review, Study, and Discussion

1. Review the differences between Jerusalem and Corinth. In what ways do these remind you of the contrasts between Christian fellowships in different locations today?

2. Note the steps which the Antioch church took to deal with the cultural issues as they arose, particularly as regards cir-

cumcision. Are there issues in the church today which are similar in nature?

3. Study the six principles for the resolution of issues related to the gospel and culture. How do you respond to these principles?

4. Think about Jesus' approach to the Sabbath-keeping traditions. How might his teaching in regard to the Sabbath be instructive to us?

Action Challenge

1. Present the ideas about cultural expressions (like layers of an onion) to a missionary who has worked with persons of a culture different from yours. Have this person compare and contrast the expressions of the two cultures.

2. Make a list of ways in which the cultural expressions in your congregation have changed in the past number of years. Has the basic worldview changed, or just the artifacts?

3. List five values in your faith which are biblically based and not affected by culture.

For Further Help

Christianity in Culture, by Charles Kraft, Orbis Books, Maryknoll, 1979. A comprehensive study of various aspects of the dynamic relationships between the gospel and culture.

A World of Difference, by Thom Hopler, InterVarsity Press, Downers Grove, Ill., 1981. A delightful description of cultural differences and how these differences affect a people's perception of the gospel.

Foolishness to the Greeks: The Gospel and Western Culture, by Lesslie Newbigin, Wm. B. Eerdmans Pub. Co., Grand Rapids, 1986. An analysis of the tensions between Western culture and the gospel. Suggestions on how the church can be faithful in its missionary task.

The Theory and Practice of Translation, by Eugene Nida and Charles R. Taber, E. J. Brill, Leiden, 1969. A fascinating study of approaches to modern Bible translation work.

Christ and Culture, by H. Richard Niebuhr, Harper and Row, New York, 1951. This book is a classic, with a presentation of the different ways in which the church relates to culture.

Chapter 8

Peoples and Places

David's Germanic grandmother used to tell him what a shock it was when her childhood congregation began to worship in the English language. She described how one of the ministers pointed out that since his Bible was written in German, most likely God himself spoke German. Another minister was confident that the wooden shingles on the roof of the church building would turn upward in dismay and grief if English was ever used for worship. In fact, within Grandmother's Pennsylvania Dutch community, when persons within the church began to live in a "worldly" manner, it was sometimes stated that they were "going English."

The transition from Pennsylvania German to English was not as catastrophic as had been feared. This congregation is still thriving after three generations of English! However, many of Grandmother's Germanic qualities have vanished in her descendants. Her forebears accurately recognized that a change in language would lead to changes in their culture. The same concern is deep-seated among most people groups. Just as the

Pennsylvania German people were concerned about maintaining their integrity, so most groups value their culture. They try to preserve the distinctive qualities within their value system which they believe have enduring meaning. In fact, recent demographic studies show that in the United States only 48 percent of the population is Anglicized, absorbed into the mainstream English culture. The remaining 52 percent consider themselves to have some other ethnic identity.

Ethnic Awareness

Two phenomena in modern North American experience have contributed significantly to the preservation of ethnic identity. First is the civil rights movement of the 1950s and 1960s. This awakening defended the right of ethnic people to be respected as equals with persons in the mainstream culture. A person did not need to be assimilated into Anglo culture in order to achieve status as an individual. *Diverse but equal* was the vision of the civil rights movement, a vision which is now a value goal of many.

A second major stream contributing to ethnic self-consciousness is the massive immigration into the United States and Canada during the last decade or so. During the 1980s, immigration numbers to the United States, legal and illegal, are reported at significantly more than one million annually. Compare this with an immigration rate of thirty thousand a year during the 1930s. These new immigrants are contributing greatly to ethnic pride and identity within the North American culture. Many of the immigrants, particularly those from Latin America, Asia, and Africa, have no intention of becoming submerged into a homogeneous Anglo culture. All our cities have become a rich mosaic of ethnic diversity. For example, in 1985 the public school system of Los Angeles was teaching in some 65 languages! In that same year, 25 American cities enjoyed the distinction of minorities being the majority.

Biblical church planting needs to be sensitive to the culture of the people groups among whom the churches are being planted. In the last chapter we examined in some depth how the gospel and culture are interrelated. Now we will focus more clearly on ways in which churches may be planted among people groups who are culturally distant from the sending church or mission agency.

Cultural Differences

The phenomenon of cultural distance is sometimes referred to as the E-1 to E-4 principle. "E" stands for evangelism; "1" is one's primary group. E-1 stands for the evangelism which flows naturally among a person's primary friends and relationships. These are the people with whom one is most comfortable and with whom one can most naturally share the gospel. In contrast, E-4 represents those who are, culturally speaking, very distant.

On David's office wall hangs a picture of a Somali nomadic family traveling with all their belongings on the backs of two camels. A remarkable feat: house, cooking utensils, beds, clothing, furniture, tied compactly on the backs of two camels. They are illiterate Muslims who have probably never seen a city.

Although David lived in Somalia for ten years, he was never able to effectively touch the nomadic community with the gospel, for they were culturally distant from him. They were E-4 people from his cultural perspective. E-2 and E-3, then, are nuances between the two extremes of those who are the closest culturally and those who are the most distant.

Some people groups are close to us culturally, and we can, with little difficulty, make ourselves understood when we attempt to communicate the gospel. Other groups, like the nomadic family pictured on the office wall, are so distant culturally that it takes special creativity and the Holy Spirit's wisdom to find ways to move into those kinds of settings with the gospel.

The Worldview of a People

Acts 17:16-34

Two considerations are necessary to share the gospel with a people group who have not yet received Jesus Christ. First we work toward forming cross-cultural teams, or preferably a team that is native to the culture of the unevangelized people. Second, we need to discover creative ways to communicate the gospel in thought forms which speak to the worldview of these unevangelized people. In chapter three, we focused on the first consideration—the formation of teams. In this chapter we will probe the relationship of the gospel to a people's worldview.

Paul was in touch with the thought forms of people groups among whom he planted churches. He was a native of Tarsus which was a center of Greek stoic philosophy. He clearly understood the worldview of the Greek philosophies and that of the polytheists. When he visited Athens, that ancient center of Greek philosophy and learning, he did a lot of listening and observing. He gained new insights into the worldview of the people. When he finally met with the philosophers on the Acropolis, he was ready to share the gospel with them in thought forms which spoke with disturbing relevance. In his message he quoted from some of their own philosophers, helping them to perceive that Jesus was the fulfillment of the quest for truth for which Greek philosophers yearned.

Some weeks later he traveled in Corinth and had the opportunity to speak in the Jewish synagogue. Here he did not refer to Greek philosophy—that was not the thought form of the Jewish people to whom he was speaking. Rather, he went right to the Old Testament and attempted to prove by the Scriptures that Jesus is the fulfillment of truth, the Messiah who is the Savior of the world.

Paul knew that Jesus Christ is good news because he is the answer to humankind's deepest questions: What is the meaning of my life? What is the meaning of death? How can I have a right relationship with the divine? How can I resolve my feelings of guilt? How can I find love and community? Whether Paul was speaking to polytheists, philosophers, or a group thoroughly acquainted with the Jewish Scriptures, he centered his message and witness on the life, death, and resurrection of Jesus. He attempted to explain the significance of Jesus within the worldview of the audience with whom he was sharing.

It is for this reason that in every situation, Paul's preaching of the gospel elicited a vigorous reaction. The people who worshiped many gods were amazed that Christians believed that Jesus alone is Lord. They gave both positive and negative responses. The Greeks could not perceive of the possibility of a resurrection of the body and some of them laughed at Paul disrespectfully. The Jews of Corinth found it incredible that the Messiah could have been crucified. In each case, Jesus Christ crucified and risen became the point of contention and division. Belief and unbelief collided.

When the gospel is presented with relevance to any worldview, it always elicits a response, whether positive or negative. Belief and unbelief become possibilities when the Word of God is heard clearly. It is never heard with clarity unless spoken within the thought forms of the people who are hearing the Word. Only then can one make an authentic decision. A division between belief and unbelief emerges as people hear the gospel as good news within their own worldviews.

Whenever a people say "yes" to the gospel, a profound transformation of their worldview begins to happen. The gospel is so revolutionary that it can never be fully at home within any human thought category. Greek philosophy perceived the body as evil and certainly as unworthy of resurrection. How different this was from the gospel revelation that a person's body, soul, and spirit are all loved and fully redeemed by God. The concept of the bodily resurrection of the dead and Greek philosophical thought forms were incompatible. When the gospel was received, it exploded the Greek worldview. The same is true of the Jewish viewpoint. Jesus just didn't fit the neat boxes into which the Jews wanted to put the Messiah. It is always so. The gospel can be fully embraced and appreciated only within the worldview which is of its own creation.

For persons who are thoroughly enmeshed in a culture or worldview, with little exposure to other ways of life, it may be quite difficult to perceive the implications of the gospel. This may be especially true for Christians in the United States who have been thoroughly enmeshed in a supposedly Christian environment and are relatively isolated from the rest of the world. Commenting on Western culture, the modern French philosopher and theologian Jacques Ellul writes, "How has it come about that the development of Christianity and the church has given birth to a society, a civilization, a culture that are completely opposite to what we read in the Bible?" (Ellul, *The Subversion of Christianity*, p. 3). It is sobering to recall that Jesus had the strongest words of condemnation for those who felt the least need to change. He seemed most gracious and accepting of those who understood their lostness and need for salvation. Would Jesus respond differently today?

We note that the American culture and worldview has been largely patterned after that of our prevailing secular culture. A growing reliance on science and technology has left more and more people unsure that the gospel has any relevance for today's world. The result is that many churches are no longer speaking a clear word about the claims of Christ. Furthermore, the dynamic, life-changing power of the gospel is often absent, replaced by endless discussion about issues which can never be resolved, or by ritual observance of the traditional religious customs.

How sad! And how far from Christ's desire to have a body which is alive and well!

Glen Yoder of Birmingham, Alabama, uses the diagrams below to illustrate (A) what has happened in many churches, and (B) what God intends to happen:

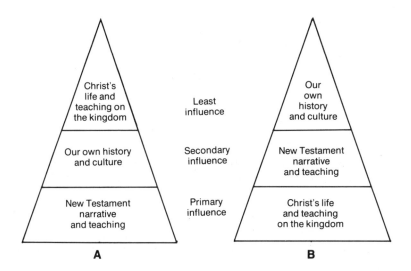

We must never fall into the trap of believing that *we* have the message for *them*—that we have nothing to learn or change. Christ warned the church at Laodicea about the dangers of self-sufficiency (Revelation 3:14-22). Those who truly follow Christ will always, to some extent, be strangers in their own culture. And they must always be ready to repent when Christ calls them to do so. Only then can they be most effective in sharing the gospel with persons of another culture.

Communicating the Gospel

Modern communication theory identifies various aspects of effective communication for response and behavior change. Charles Kraft from the Fuller School of World Mission, in his book *Christianity in Culture*, identifies several basic components of effective communication. These include:

1) *Communication must be specific.* The reality which one is communicating must be observable and touchable. This is why much advertising includes specific testimonies. Jesus, God with

us, is a specific event. The local congregation is specific, and so is the testimony of a Christian. People need to "see," "hear," "touch," and "handle" the gospel (1 John 1:1).

2) *Good communication must be a surprise.* The advertisements we remember are those which astonish us. The gospel is the supreme surprise! To perceive that God loves us enough to suffer for us, to realize that he invites us to become his sons and daughters, to see the church ministering in compassion and love—these are good news surprises.

3) *Communication needs to be receptor-, or listener-, oriented.* People will respond only if they understand what is said and believe it is relevant to their needs. The angel told Mary that her son Jesus would be Immanuel, which, *when interpreted,* means "God with us." The church planting team needs to prayerfully and creatively *interpret* Jesus as the one who ministers with relevance to the needs of the person.

4) *Communication should be discovery-oriented.* There is a touch of mystery in the gospel, an invitation to discover. Jesus never announced that he is the Son of God, although he did confess it when he was asked. Rather than proclaim himself as divine or the Messiah, he invited people to discover the mystery of his person and mission for themselves.

5) *Communication invites decision.* "Go to your auto dealer today!" we are urged. Jesus' presence, teaching, and ministry always confronted people with decision. As church planters minister and witness, they need to invite decision. Like Jesus, the team should become a sign of the great divide which Christ creates whenever he is present. The Holy Spirit and the church planter partner in calling people to a decision.

6) *Communication should affirm the dignity of the person.* "You deserve Sophia perfume," purrs the advertiser. In a rather different way, Jesus also affirmed people: children, prostitutes, lepers, beggars, fishermen, farmers, tax collectors, sinners, and even publicans. People were attracted to Jesus by his affirming spirit. Similarly, church planters do not condemn

people. Rather, they extend the surprising invitation, "You are welcome to become part of the joyous, loving family of God!" (Charles Kraft, *Christianity in Culture*, pp. 173-178)

Contextual Response

The way the gospel speaks is always different, for the good news needs to be involved in ongoing dialogue with the local culture and local perceptions.

For example, the teaching that a Christian should turn the other cheek when an enemy strikes on one cheek may make a lot of sense to a Hindu pacifist who sees this as being in tune with the Jain doctrine of *ahimsa*. However, for a black South African who has experienced racial discrimination, this teaching may seem to be bad news, a suggestion that one should simply acquiesce to injustice and evil. Especially in the light of Bishop Desmond Tutu's leadership, the "other cheek" teaching might well be further developed by the story of Jesus cleansing the temple. This story suggests that nonviolent confrontation with evil is also appropriate in some circumstances. This is not to suggest there is a conflict between these two approaches to the enemy. Both are nonviolent, but there is a difference in approach, depending on the context.

For the Kekchi Indians in the highlands of Guatemala, the gospel will often be heard primarily as the good news that Jesus is risen and has triumphed over the evil spirits. For the childless wife of a farmer in the Congo Valley, the gospel may be heard as the good news that barren women will also go to heaven, the news that children contribute nothing to one's salvation. To the secularist in Massachusetts who has always lived within a naturalistic framework, the gospel may become the good news that God loves and cares for people and wants to become personally involved in one's life. For the Hindus in Madras who have always believed that human life is a tragedy—that history is a cycle of meaninglessness—the gospel is the good news that life *is eternally meaningful*. History is destined for a marvelous consummation when the kingdom of God is fulfilled. Although the presence of Jesus is always disturbing, he is also the best news people have ever heard.

Although we need to attempt to interpret Jesus Christ within the worldview of the people among whom we witness, we must also realize that Jesus himself is his own best interpreter. This is because the gospel is not a philosophical system. Rather it is the account of God's saving acts in history and his supreme act in Jesus. Whenever a person meets and responds to Jesus, that person begins to discover for herself *the surprise* of Jesus within her own worldview.

David's ministry as an overseas missions director enables him to hear Jesus preached from many different cultural pulpits. He is always "surprised" by fresh insights concerning Jesus, which never occurred to him before.

For example, a Dyak chief in the riverine jungles of West Kalimantan said," Jesus is good news to us because he has delivered us from the fear of the birds!" For these peoples the birds were thought to be omens from the spirits. Christ had freed them from the power of the avian omens!

The gospel is always relevant and always graciously revolutionary. The gospel speaks with power within each respective worldview, while at the same time transforming that worldview. The gospel is always good news that is surprising, confrontational, and inviting.

Some people groups and their worldview seem more receptive to the gospel than others. Paul stayed only a few days in Athens, but lived nearly two years in Corinth. In Athens the initial response had been so disappointing that Paul, in dismay, decided to move on to Corinth. There the Lord revealed to him that many people would believe (Acts 18:5-11). He apparently stayed longer among the people groups who were responsive than among those who seemed quite disinterested.

Noting Paul's example, some people believe that church planting efforts should focus primarily on people groups who seem responsive. Others point out that the apparently unresponsive may never perceive the gospel if no one takes the time to interpret and reinterpret patiently the good news. This question forms the basis for considerable debate among modern missionaries and church planters.

Jesus Surprised a Stranger!

John 4:1-42

One outstanding example of proclaiming the gospel within a people group is recorded in John 4—Jesus preaching the good news among the Samaritans. In this case, Jesus made a specific decision to break out of the normal routine of his Jewish circle of witness in order to meet people who were ostracized from mainstream Jewish culture. They were the Samaritans.

Not only did Jesus do the nonconventional thing by passing through Samaria, but he also spoke with a woman who was despised by her own community. She came to get water at noon, which is not the time Middle Eastern women draw water. She had apparently alienated herself from her community by sexually enticing the husbands of other women in the town, so she needed to draw water alone. Thus it was that she met Jesus at the well at noon. He surprised her by asking for water. By this request, Jesus demonstrated a basic principle of communicating the gospel cross-culturally: accept a gift from the people to whom you are going to minister. The woman was astonished, but obviously pleased with the opportunity of sharing her water with this Jewish gentleman.

As the conversation unfolded, Jesus helped her to perceive that she needed to receive Messiah into the center of her worldview—into the center of her life. The symbolism of their conversation all had to do with worldview. The well which Jacob dug was the symbol of her history and her tradition. The mountain on which the Samaritans conducted sacrifices was, according to their ancient legends, the very spot at which Adam and Eve first set foot on earth when they were created.

The woman asked, "Should we worship at this mountain or Jerusalem?" meaning, "Which is best, David's city or Adam's mountain?"

This was a question with explosive implications for a Jew and a Samaritan meeting at the well. That question went right to the core of the Jewish versus the Samaritan worldview and their respective identities. Even today, Samaritans offer sacrifices on Adam's mountain and Jews worship at the old temple wall, known as the wailing wall in Jerusalem.

Jesus gently helped the woman see that "Jerusalem" or "the mountain" are of no ultimate consequence. Her real need was to meet Messiah and invite him right into the center of her whole worldview and her life. She needed to believe him who is the Messiah, who can minister forgiveness to her guilt, give healing to her life, and call out living water from the center of her being.

Redemption happened to that woman as she talked with Jesus. She raced back into the village, a free woman. The load of guilt lifted. She called all in the village to come to meet the one who had revealed her innermost thoughts—the one who had transformed her burdened spirit into song and freedom and praise. By evening, many of the villagers believed in Jesus.

Homogeneous Unit Principle

For many years, the School of World Mission at Fuller Theological Seminary, under the leadership of Donald McGavran, has been teaching the homogeneous unit principle. These missionary trainers have recognized that people often become Christians most readily when introduced to Christ by someone much like themselves. The homogeneous unit principle recognizes that people feel more comfortable among others of their own group. Sometimes whole villages come to Christ after a prominent leader in the community takes the first step, even though the village may have resisted a missionary's effort for years. Why? Because one of their "own people" has become involved. For this reason, in some situations churches may grow most rapidly when there are large concentrations of the same kind of people within the neighborhood. For example, the Hmong people are refugees living in a three-county area in southeastern Pennsylvania. Nearly all have become active members of the Hmong Alliance Church at Hinkletown. Within six years of the beginning of this congregation, only one family out of about 100 was not yet a member of this thriving fellowship. Although these kinds of churches may grow rapidly, they often find it difficult to assimilate others. There are many examples of this phenomenon in North America. For example, the Coptic Church or some of the Lutheran and Reformed groups who possess a significant sense of ethnic identity.

Some groups move beyond ethnic identity and become genuinely diverse. Others seem to maintain ethnic identity for generations. In the past, Mennonite and Amish congregations within North and South America have been examples of these two movements. In most Amish and Mennonite congregations, there has been a strong emphasis on common heritage as well as on uniform patterns of dress, worship style, and patterns of family living. In more recent times, there has been an increasing diversity within the Mennonite church because of evangelistic outreach. In fact, in 1980 the Mennonite church worshiped in about 100 languages in 40 countries around the world, with a dazzling diversity of peoples. The trend toward diversity continues to this day.

In contrast, most Amish congregations continue to reflect a rather uniform pattern. One factor which has kept Amish congregations united is their retention of the German language mentioned at the beginning of this chapter. Persons who do not speak the Pennsylvania German dialect are naturally not attracted to worship services conducted in the German language.

In the same way, various other people groups in the United States tend to enjoy worshiping in a congregation which largely reflects their interest in a uniform language and culture. This has always been true of many of the Eastern Orthodox groups when they migrate to lands away from home. Language group churches, such as Chinese-speaking congregations, are unlikely to attract a person who speaks only Spanish or English. For this reason, many first-generation immigrants to the United States or other countries are attracted to a congregation which worships in a language and cultural style like that of their mother country.

As long as new immigrants come to be a part of the church, language group or ethnic churches can flourish. However, the second or third generation of such immigrants are assimilated into the primary culture, and will often be attracted to churches which reflect a greater diversity of practice. Language and ethnic group churches need to be exceptionally creative in order to provide for the needs of their members who desire to worship with a congregation which embodies diversity. In urban settings it is often possible for several ethnic and language group churches to worship in the same building with an "assimilation" congregation. By careful cooperation they can all benefit from both the strengths of the homogeneous unit principle and the attractions of diversity.

Social class and economic status are also factors which draw together certain persons, to the exclusion of others. Donald McGavran and his associates have often been criticized because their teaching seems to justify segregated congregations who only minister to a narrow scope of the population, without interest in others who have great needs. Because of this criticism, they have modified their teaching to say that a congregation should reflect the diversity within its own immediate community. In this way it may still be homogeneous with the community, but not to the exclusion of the persons around them who need ministry.

In a pluralistic society like North America or in most large cities around the world, it is desirable to plant both homogeneous people group churches *and* heterogeneous churches which are highly diverse in ethnic composition. Furthermore, it is never right to exclude any true believers from the church of their choice. No congregation is a true colony of heaven on earth if it denies membership to a person because of racial, ethnic, language, social, educational, or economic considerations. That fact is central to the New Testament understanding and expression of church. At the same time, it is right for people to worship in the language and idiom of their choice. It is for this reason that we believe it is both biblical and wise, especially in urban settings, to plant both heterogeneous and homogeneous congregations. We also believe it is wise for all of the diverse congregations in a region or city to plan and cooperate together in mission. Cooperation between diverse congregations helps all to experience enrichment, and it is a sign in the community of the unity in Christ which characterizes the kingdom of God.

Laser Approach

A variety of means have been used by churches and mission agencies to reach out to different people groups. The Southern Baptists often speak of a "laser approach" to ministry among people groups. In the technological world, a laser is used to perform surgery or perform other tasks which require an extremely concentrated focus of energy. In the same way, the Southern Baptists believe that certain people groups can be most effectively reached by a church planter who focuses ministry on a specific people group. Furthermore, they believe that the church planter should be able to identify closely with the target group. Thus, if they are attempting to reach the Chinese population, they recruit a person who speaks Chinese, even if this person has had no previous Baptist affiliation. If a group has *no* Christians, the laser approach will focus on evangelizing persons in the group who have leadership potential. If persons respond to Christ, these potential leaders should be encouraged to prepare for pastoral church planting among their own people. The Southern Baptists find this approach to be more effective than trying to find a church planter who would need to bridge a culture gap in order to minister to the target group.

Urban Evangelism

One effective way to evangelize people groups is by planting churches in the cities. Most modern urban centers consist of a mosaic of peoples. Each of these people groups have connections with their own home community. Thus by planting a church among the Garifuna in New York City, their kinfolk in the coastlands of Belize and Honduras are also encouraged to follow Christ. Letters, visits, and modern mobility makes it likely that when an urban people group responds to the gospel, their kinsfolk even in distant places will eventually also hear the gospel. Furthermore, urban peoples are often more open to new beliefs and patterns of life. Personal freedom is greater in the city. For these reasons, urban people groups are sometimes much more receptive to the gospel than their kinfolk in the rural hinterland.

Jesus recognized the strategic significance of the city for world and people group evangelism. For this reason, he informed his disciples in his farewell words that their witness would begin in Jerusalem. Remember that Jerusalem was nearly 200 miles from home for the Galilean peasants who formed Jesus' inner circle of disciples. These leaders were not very comfortable with the city. In fact, it was in this Jerusalem that Jesus had been sentenced and crucified only weeks before. Nevertheless, now Jesus was telling them that their ministry was to begin in the city.

They obeyed the command of Jesus, and Pentecost happened in the city, where the church was born. From the great city of Jerusalem, the church spread to other cities, people groups, and countries. Over a dozen languages or regions are mentioned in Acts 2. The story of the book of Acts is the story of urban evangelism. The church moved from city to city: Samaria, Damascus, Antioch, Caesarea, Lystra, Philippi, Thessalonica, Athens, Corinth, Ephesus, Derbe, Rome, and many other cities as well. A kaleidoscope of peoples comprised these cities. No wonder Jesus commissioned his disciples to begin in the city. They took that command seriously.

The city is the place where people meet. Churches which thrive in cities touch the entire countryside, because in the city is a kaleidoscope of cultures, peoples, businesses, philosophies, and travelers. Cities are the centers of power—economic, political, cultural, religious, and educational. Cities are the change agents of the nations. Churches planted in cities touch the heartbeat of an entire region.

Churches in the countryside tend to be ethnic churches. Almost everyone attending a country church comes from the same kind of background. While there are also ethnic churches in the city, many urban congregations face the continual challenge of forming a new community from people who have never been involved in community together. Both homogeneous and heterogeneous churches thrive in the city. In Antioch when Jews and Greeks, rich and poor, slaves and free people, persons from Asia, Europe and Africa, all met together in unity and fellowship, it was a miracle which only God could bring about. In the ancient world there was no precedent anywhere for a community of such diversity. Thus, the multiethnic church in the city became a special kind of revelation of the nature of the gospel and the new community of reconciliation which God was creating through Christ.

Ignorance, exploitation, and an independent spirit thrive in the city. Orphans live on the street and male and female prostitutes stand on street corners. Drug addicts look for pleasure through chemical stimulation. The unemployed seek work, while the wealthy bask in luxury. Crowded rooms and spacious mansions are found in the same city. Many are homeless and hungry. Cities are places of extreme loneliness and alienation for many people.

Jesus wept over the city. Christ's compassion needs to be revealed to the people of the city through the church.

An Urban Explosion

Today the city is with us more than ever before. When the American Declaration of Independence was signed, 5 percent of the inhabitants of the thirteen colonies were urban. Now, over 75 percent of the North American people are urban. That same trend is evident worldwide. In 1950, 28 percent of the world's population was urban. By 1975, the percentage of urban persons had risen to 41 percent. By the year 2000, 55 percent of the world's population will likely be urban. That will be 3.5 billion city dwellers worldwide! One-and-a-quarter million new people are becoming city dwellers each week!

This phenomenal movement is creating mega-cities. In Jesus' day, cities of a hundred thousand were considered large. Now, during the latter part of the twentieth century, there are ten metropolitan centers in the world with a population of over ten million. It is anticipated that by the year 2000, there will be seven urban areas with populations of from twenty to thirty million. In fact, the population of Mexico City may well exceed thirty million by the year 2000.

What does this mean for evangelism? First, the sheer numbers are overwhelming. In order to make a significant impact on the urban masses, one must think in much greater numbers than ever before. This does not necessarily mean huge churches, but it does mean that many more workers are needed.

Second, the urban frontier brings with it the technological society, with the accompanying information explosion. The age of telecommunications requires appropriate adaptations to the way we share the gospel. The institutional church has often been too slow to adapt to creative means of sharing the gospel.

With each new step forward in media development, the church has lagged behind the more creative Christian entrepreneurs. We need to call out those among us who can effectively share the gospel with urban professionals and neopagan people.

Along with the explosion of knowledge and wealth which accompanies urban expansion and development, comes the blight of the urban poor. A steadily increasing number of jobless and homeless people are crying for relief. The command of Christ to preach the gospel to the poor is as relevant as it was in the first century.

If Jesus was concerned that his disciples focus their first church planting efforts in the city, how much more he must desire this for our world today? The cities of the last years of the twentieth century are the principal church planting frontiers. Every city block of every city on earth deserves to have at least one resident cluster of loving, witnessing Christians. Surely every people and language group in every city deserves at least one thriving cluster of redeemed people who point the way to salvation. Surely the Spirit of God desires to create at least one cluster of vibrant, witnessing Christians in every apartment complex. God has blessed this simple vision and plan in Seoul, Korea, where cells of believers throughout that city comprise a church of over half a million people.

In order to evangelize the cities today, we must return to the New Testament model of urban evangelism. The approach used was to plant house churches or cell groups throughout entire metropolitan regions. Every urban congregation should be in the cell group planting business. We need to pray for the multiplication of congregations and cell groups in apartment buildings and city blocks in urban areas. This is the model which Christian leaders in Birmingham have begun. Denominations are partnering together. The goal is to plant simultaneously at least 50 thriving congregations of 300 members each. Each of these 50 congregations consists of many house churches or cell groups. The goal is to form at least one cell group in every neighborhood in Birmingham. They hope to move the entire city for God through this broad-based cooperation in church planting.

The task is urgent. The faithful church which is exalting Jesus Christ is the best news any city could ever receive.

Urgency!

Matthew 28:19

Jesus took the time and special effort to communicate the gospel of the kingdom to the Samaritan people. In the same way, he commissioned his disciples to go from people to people and to the city proclaiming the gospel, making disciples of all peoples. The "nations" referred to in Christ's great commission are the people groups of the world, not nations as we think of the geographical or political boundaries today. In fact, the original Greek word is *ethnos*, from which we derive the English word *ethnic*. Jesus desired that the gospel be preached to every ethnic group. In fact, just before his death Jesus asserted that history would not be complete until the gospel was proclaimed to all nations as a testimony to all people (Matthew 24:14). Church planting among the peoples of the earth is apparently the most important vocation possible. Only as the gospel is proclaimed and heard among all peoples can history come to its conclusion. Taking the gospel to people who have not yet heard the good news is central in God's design for bringing about the consummation of history in glory.

If these were the ideas of a theologian or a philosopher they would seem arrogant and unrealistic. However, these are none other than the words of Jesus. In humility we accept the incredible mandate to proclaim the gospel among all peoples. With deep gratitude and joy we recognize that as the gospel is received and takes root among the peoples, the day comes nearer and nearer when Jesus will return to earth and bring to glorious conclusion the drama of history.

The U.S. Center for World Mission and Change the World

Ministries put special emphasis on prayer intercession for people groups around the world. Research at the U.S. Center shows there are about 16,000 people groups around the world with little or no gospel witness native to their language and culture. Their monthly *Global Prayer Digest* is a daily prayer guide for intercession for people who have no church, or have not heard the Gospel with sufficient clarity to believe in Jesus.

Change the World Ministries publishes a world map which is a guide to prayer for the leaders of nations of the world. In addition, this organization publishes a monthly prayer bulletin listing a daily prayer focus. Using these prayer guides may be one of the best ways to help persons become familiar with the people groups around the world, and gain a burden and vision for evangelizing these peoples.

Revelation 5:9-10; 21:1-4

The apostle John saw a vision from the island of Patmos which summarizes all the themes of this chapter. He saw a vision of a great throng singing praises to the Lamb. These multitudes of singing people came from every tribe and nation and language. He saw a vision of churches—redeemed people—planted among every people group on earth. He saw a vision of a great city, the new Jerusalem, the bride of the Lamb, the city to which the peoples came for healing. What joy was in evidence as thousands upon thousands of clusters of redeemed people sang praises to the Lamb—Jesus our Savior and Lord! In fact, the whole universe began to rejoice, and before long every creature in heaven and earth and all the angels were joining in the great song of praise to the Lamb who has redeemed men and women for God from every people group.

For Review, Study, and Discussion

1. Do you represent a people group other than the mainstream culture in which you find yourself? How was Christ first presented to your "people"?

2. Reflect on the idea that the worldview of a people group is always transformed by the gospel. Are there ways in which your "people" have yet to respond to some aspect of the gospel?

3. How did Jesus demonstrate sensitivity to "people groups"?

4. How did the Apostle Paul and his church planting team adapt to the various people groups they encountered in ministry?

5. Review the authors' suggestions for ways in which the gospel may be communicated effectively for response and behavior change. Do you agree or disagree with these suggestions? What other suggestions might you have for communicating good news?

6. What is your response to the homogeneous unit principle? Is your church consciously ethnic in its social makeup?

Action Challenge

1. Contact your local or denominational mission committee or agency to find out what people groups you are reaching. Are plans being made to reach out to any new groups?

2. Obtain a listing of people groups and begin to pray daily for those groups which God directs you to intercede for.

3. What people groups are represented in your community? Within 15 minutes' driving distance of your church facility? Is someone sharing the gospel with these groups? If not, ask God for direction concerning ways to reach out to them.

For Further Help

Change the World Ministries, P.O. Box 58338, Mission Hills, Calif.

Unleashing the Church, by Frank Tillapaugh, Regal Books, 1985. The story of church ministries through the affirmation of the many gifts and vision of the congregation.

U.S. Center for World Mission, 1605 Elizabeth Street,

Pasadena, Calif. (818-797-1111), which publishes the *Global Prayer Digest.*

Christianity in Culture, by Charles Kraft, Orbis Books, Maryknoll, 1979.

Heirs of the Same Promise, by Wesley Balda, Missionary Advanced Research and Communication Center, MARC, 1984. An inspirational description of the common heritage of God's peoples.

Urban Ministry, by David Claerbaut, Zondervan, Grand Rapids, 1983. A study of the modern urban phenomenon with practical approaches to urban ministry.

The Subversion of Christianity, by Jacques Ellul, Eerdmans, Grand Rapids, 1986. A scholarly description of the fact and the causes of the differences between biblical faith and Western Christianity.

The First Urban Christians, by Wayne Meeks, Yale University Press, New Haven, London, 1983. A study of church development in the cities of the first century.

The Social Setting of Pauline Christianity, by Gerd Theissen, Fortress Press, Philadelphia, 1982. A scholarly analysis of the Corinthian church as a case study of early urban Christian experience.

Chapter 9

Discipling
and Training

In 1979, Richard and Lois Landis and their three teenage sons moved to Stratford, New Jersey, to plant a church. They knew no one in the community. To make acquaintances, they sometimes went to a local fast food restaurant. Richard would take his tray to a table, asking if he could join the person or persons sitting there, and Lois would take her tray to another. Slowly they developed acquaintances. A Bible fellowship began in their home, and through the power of the Holy Spirit, people were converted and a congregation was formed. Within six years, Word Fellowship in Stratford, New Jersey, became a congregation of about 250 on a Sunday morning. This church is now planting another congregation and is also helping to extend the gospel of the kingdom overseas.

A factor central to the growth of the Word Fellowship congregation is Richard Landis's commitment to training faithful men. Within a year of the beginning of the Word Fellowship congregation, he had already identified several persons whom he believed were gifted for leadership. Week after week he invested his life in these men, like Jesus, working closely with this cluster of potential pastors and leaders.

Many of these men had no previous experience in a Christian church. They were biblically illiterate. Faithfully, Richard taught them the Bible and helped them understand Christian disciplines. They worked together at learning how to be Christian fathers and husbands. They learned prayer together and worked with the pastor in Christian ministry.

In 1983 one of these men shared with the team that he and his wife believed the Lord was calling them to be a church planter couple in Atlantic City. This couple was Charles and Donna Arnold, mentioned in chapter seven. Several years before, the Holy Spirit had graciously rescued Charles and Donna from a life of deep sin. In gratitude for what the Lord Jesus had done for them, they shared with the leadership of the Word Fellowship congregation the call burning in their hearts: to go to Atlantic City.

The congregation confirmed their call. The Arnolds went to a Bible institute for one year to strengthen their biblical and pastoral skills. Then they, and their two children, Mary Ann and Charles, were commissioned by the Word Fellowship congregation to go to Atlantic City to plant a church.

Richard Landis visits with the Arnolds regularly for encouragement, counsel, and prayer. The other leaders in training at Word Fellowship also visit Atlantic City frequently. In this way they are also learning how to plant a church through the example of the Arnold family. Most significantly, people intercede in constant prayer for the ministry in Atlantic City. Richard and Lois Landis and the team around them are persons schooled in the ministry of prayer. In their whole approach to leadership, they consciously follow the patterns for discipling exemplified in the book of Acts.

Acts 17:1-9; 1 Thessalonians 1:2-10

Wherever Paul went, he made disciples. He introduced

people to Jesus Christ and showed them how to be true followers of Christ. In some instances he stayed only a short time in one place. Often he had only limited time to teach the basics of commitment to Christ. For example, in Thessalonica he stayed only a few weeks. However, they developed a model congregation. In fact, Paul says to them in his letter, "You became a model to all the believers in Macedonia and Achaia—your faith in God has become known everywhere." What an affirmation of faith! How did Paul, in a few short weeks, lead these people to such faith in Christ?

One of the earliest of Paul's letters was written to the Thessalonian church. The insights below come from Paul's first letter to them.

1. *Paul came with the power of the Holy Spirit.* He did not simply depend on words to convey the message of the gospel, but on the power of the gospel, expressed by the Holy Spirit, resulting in deep conviction (1:5).

2. *Paul cared deeply for them.* He shared his life with them and invested a great deal of time in them. As a father exhorts his children, and as a mother nurses her young, Paul dealt with them (2:7-12).

3. *They responded by becoming disciples.* In response to Paul's message, they became imitators of Paul and the Lord. Furthermore, they became imitators of the established churches in Judea. By observing and following the pattern of life they observed in Paul and others, they also grew to be mature disciples. This qualified them to be a model for others (1:6-7; 2:14).

4. *Paul kept in touch with them.* Paul was driven away from Thessalonica because of strong persecution. He was so concerned about them that he sent Timothy to encourage them as Paul was prevented from going on several occasions (2:17-18; 3:1-2,6).

5. *Paul kept praying for them.* Paul indicates that he prayed earnestly night and day for the Thessalonians (3:9-10).

Paul's work among the Thessalonians is discipleship training at its best. By the Lord's grace, this young church even withstood the heat of persecution without the presence of an apostle or any other strong leader. Perhaps this example can teach us a valuable lesson in discipleship. Basic training for Christian living may be completed in a matter of weeks if certain factors are present.

What basics must a new believer learn in order to be a true disciple or to move into leadership training? Perhaps the writer to the Hebrews has the answer for us.

Basics of Christian Living

Hebrews 5:11-14; 6:1-3

In this passage, the writer laments that his readers are slow to learn. These persons are like children who require milk, which is easily digested. They are not prepared to deal with solid food. According to chapter six, there are six foundational understandings which the Hebrews had not yet mastered: (1) repentance from sin, (2) faith in God, (3) baptism, (4) laying on of hands, (5) the resurrection of the dead, and (6) eternal judgment. Apparently, the writer expected them to learn these quickly, then move on to maturity. As expressed in Hebrews 5:14, maturity is measured by one's ability to live effectively as a Christian and teach others to do so.

Like the Hebrews addressed in this letter, many modern Christians are content to be taught the basics over and over again, without ever developing the ability to make disciples of other people. It is a sobering thought to consider that one of the clearest marks of a disciple is the ability to make disciples. This was the case in Thessalonica, and it is still true today.

Paul Trained Disciples to Become Leaders

Acts 16:1-10

When Paul left his home congregation in Antioch for his second effort of planting churches among the Gentiles, he stopped at Lystra in Central Turkey. Here he had nearly lost his life on his first church planting journey. The people tried to stone him to death when he was preaching. Nevertheless, Paul was not afraid to return to Lystra.

While visiting this new church, he met a young man named Timothy. The church in Lystra highly recommended this youth who had a Gentile father and a Jewish mother. Perhaps Timothy himself had seen Paul nearly stoned to death at the climax of the church planting effort in Lystra many months before. Timothy seemed to have a keen appreciation for Paul. He was a vivacious youth and saw in Paul and his vision a goal worth dying for. He was not dismayed nor discouraged by the dangers and challenges involved in church planting.

So when Paul left Lystra, Timothy went with him. The church apparently encouraged Timothy in this commitment. Most likely this man of character was eager to learn from Paul the gifts of pastoral leadership and the church planting ministry.

For several years, Timothy learned from Paul by watching him work and by assisting him in his work. He was with Paul in Philippi when they met with Lydia and the women at the river. He saw these women responding in faith to Jesus when Paul shared his evangelistic witness. He was with Paul when the slave girl mocked Paul in the marketplaces of Philippi. Later, he watched Paul cast out the evil spirit from her. When the Philippian business community became outraged and a tremendous riot developed, Timothy was with Paul. He witnessed Paul being beaten and imprisoned, and he saw God's miraculous intervention in the earthquake. He rejoiced at the subsequent conversion of the whole household of the Philippian jailer. In all these experiences Timothy watched Paul and worked with him. He *saw* and he *did* ministry in partnership with Paul not only in Philippi, but in subsequent church planting in other cities. It is not surprising that Timothy became an effective minister and overseer of the church.

Acts 19:8-12

Earlier in this chapter, we noted that Paul sometimes stayed in one location for a couple of weeks or months, and then pressed on to begin a new ministry. That is only part of the story. He also put his roots into communities where it was necessary for the church to be firmly established. One such community was Ephesus. Paul invested three full years in that city. What could Paul have been doing for three years in Ephesus?

Paul taught. He opened a Bible institute in the Hall of Tyrannus. People came to this Bible institute from throughout Asia Minor. Consequently, we read that the Word of God grew mightily throughout the whole region.

While teaching in the Bible institute, Paul was also actively committed to developing a thriving congregation in Ephesus. His first encounter in Ephesus was with twelve persons who had inaccurate knowledge of the gospel. They had heard of John the Baptist and had been baptized by Apollos, an Egyptian evangelist. Priscilla and Aquila, partners with Paul, explained the way of Christ more accurately to Apollos. Paul himself met with these twelve persons and led them into the experience of the full truth which is revealed in Jesus Christ. They were baptized by the Holy Spirit, thereby establishing the foundation for a thriving church in Ephesus. For the next two years, Paul continued his teaching ministry in this developing congregation. He was vigorously involved in evangelism. He exercised his teaching gift in the Hall of Tyrannus, enriched through his own practical experience in church planting.

The Ephesus "Bible Institute" must have been an exceedingly exciting experience. Students, probably believers and nonbelievers, may have traveled 500 miles and more to learn from Paul. Many traveled on foot to hear this veteran teacher expound the Word of God. They were introduced to the gospel. By watching Paul in action, believers learned how to pray, how to evangelize, and how to pastor a congregation. Undoubtedly, he occasionally took his students with him into the marketplaces to assist him in evangelistic conversations. In this way, they developed the pastoral and evangelistic skills needed to extend the kingdom throughout all of Asia Minor.

It is also obvious that the curriculum of the teaching ministry in Ephesus included much more than observation and practice. Solid biblical theology was also communicated to the students. Presumably, the book of Romans was written at this time, and it may well be that the careful theological presentation developed in the book of Romans is the "fleshing-out" of classroom lecture notes. This letter is a systematic theology, anchored in the Old Testament as fulfilled in Jesus Christ. It is also keenly sensitive to the philosophical and ethical issues of Christian faith and lifestyle.

Students probably came and spent a period of time with Paul in his school and in the ministry in Ephesus. Then they returned to their homes, putting into practice what they had learned. Later they went back to the retreat center in Ephesus for further inspiration and teaching in the way of Christ. Thus, there was the constant rhythm between the actual practice of ministry in their home community and learning in the school which Paul conducted.

Previously we described riots throughout the city at the end of Paul's teaching ministry in Ephesus. These riots revealed the tremendous conflict taking place between the power of the gospel and the powers that opposed Christ. What an unforgettable example of power encounter Paul's students must have observed!

Acts 20:1-6

When Paul left Ephesus, he took with him a cluster of persons to visit some of the churches which he had planted in Macedonia and Greece. We may assume that these persons were leaders he had trained in Ephesus. He wanted them to see the churches he had told them about in his church planting classes. These persons included Sopater, Aristarchus, Secundus, Gaius, Timothy, Tychicus, and Trophimus. He wanted these leaders experienced in church development in Asia also to experience Christian fellowship in European churches. This journey was a cross-cultural church planting field trip for the leaders whom Paul was training.

Principles of Leadership Training

Let us summarize the principles which Paul used in leadership training for church planting.

1. *The teacher must be a model and an example to the leaders-in-training.* They must be able to see the teacher performing the ministry which they will be emulating.

2. *All training needs to include in-service experience.* Emerging leaders must have the opportunity to do ministry in the presence of their teacher. As they minister, the leader gives counsel on how to improve what they are doing, and also gives them encouragement.

3. *Training also involves systematic theological teaching.* Good leaders need to have a good theological base. A solid grounding in the Bible and good acquaintance with the philosophical and cultural issues which the faithful church confronts are all vitally important disciplines for an effective church planter and pastor.

4. *The church planter should have cross-cultural field trip exposure* in congregations developing in other kinds of cultural settings. We gain new perspectives when we meet Christians from other cultures.

These four dimensions of effective leadership training were beautifully intertwined in Paul's teaching ministry in Ephesus, and in his leadership training commitment to Timothy.

The Teacher Keeps in Contact

1 Timothy 1:1-5; 2 Timothy 1:1-7; Titus 1:1-5

Of course we are aware that Paul's training ministry needed

to come to an end. Shortly after his three years of teaching in the Ephesus "Bible Institute," Paul was in prison, his public teaching ministry severely curtailed. Nevertheless, Paul kept in constant contact with the persons he had trained for ministry. He wrote two letters to Timothy. He encouraged him to stir up the gift which had been affirmed within him through the laying on of hands. He counseled Timothy on the way in which he should conduct his ministry. His letters encouraged Timothy and upheld him. He wrote in the same manner to Titus. He told him to be bold in his witness to the gospel. These letters explicitly demonstrate that Paul stayed in contact with those he had trained for ministry. What an encouragement that must have been to these younger men!

In every one of the letters to the churches, Paul mentioned specific persons for greeting and encouragement. Most likely these were people he had helped to train in ministry in their respective congregations. Probably he had personally laid hands on these persons and set them aside for the work of eldering and pastoring in the different churches he had established. He remembered them by name in his letters and affirmed their ministry by words of encouragement which were read in the presence of the whole congregation.

The Teacher Prays!

Paul's letters also revealed something else. He interceded continuously in prayer on behalf of the persons whom he had trained and commissioned for ministry. Even when in prison, month after month and year after year, Paul never forgot to pray for the leaders he had trained. Where did Paul catch this vision of ceaseless prayer for these leaders? He got it from Jesus himself. Jesus spent nights in prayer for his disciples. On one occasion when Peter was near being destroyed by the evil one, Jesus assured him, "I have prayed for you." What an encouragement that must have been to Peter.

Thus, we see that the mission of the church planter is not

only to call and train leaders, but also to follow those leaders with prayer.

Jesus Equipped His Disciples for Church Planting
Matthew 5:1-16; Luke 6:12-16, 40

Paul's strategy for leadership training is not unlike that of Jesus. At the beginning of his ministry, Jesus invested much time in prayer, then called twelve men whom he commissioned to be apostles. For the next three years, Jesus used the same training approaches for his disciples as Paul later used for those whom he was training. Jesus modeled leadership. He provided opportunities for the apostles and for many other disciples, as well, to practice ministry. He taught them the nature of the kingdom. He also provided field trips for them, including several journeys into Gentile communities where they could see firsthand the cross-cultural relevance of the gospel of the kingdom.

Jesus was aware that he could not teach everyone with equal intensity. Yet Jesus had a mission—the establishment of the church in such a way that it would be equipped to extend to the ends of the earth. Since he himself could not go to the ends of the earth, he focused on training twelve leaders. Of course, he also taught others as the opportunity presented itself. But his primary focus was on training twelve persons to carry on the mission after his ministry on earth was completed.

Tradition tells us that after Jesus' ascension to heaven, one of the apostles, namely Matthew, took the gospel into the region of Mesopotamia, planting churches throughout the area. Another strong tradition indicates that the apostle Thomas traveled to India and planted churches there, one of which is known today as the Mar Thoma Church. The church of South India traces its spiritual lineage back to the apostle Thomas. Yet another tradition tells us that Mark, who had worked closely with the apostle Peter, went to Egypt and planted a church in that nation. There is also the strong tradition that Peter went on to Rome and served as a church planter in that city for a time. Jesus faithfully trained leaders who took the gospel into areas which he could never have reached in a single lifetime.

Every church planter should do the same. Not only is he commissioned to plant a church, but also to train men and women in apostolic ministry to go out from the congregation to extend the gospel into regions beyond. This needs to be a foundational commitment of every church planter: plant churches and train others to do the same.

Matthew 28:16-20

Jesus emphasized the close relationship between church formation and discipleship training in his last commission to the disciples before his ascension. These verses, which contain the "great commission," have often been used to emphasize the importance of sending missionaries to foreign lands. A careful look at the structure of the verse, however, reveals a slightly different emphasis. In most modern translations of the Bible, the central emphasis of the verse is to make disciples among all peoples. The ideas of going, baptizing, and teaching, all relate to the central thrust of disciplemaking.

Disciplemaking Today

James Nikkel, an experienced Canadian church planter and evangelist, uses an example from the field of athletics to illustrate an important aspect of disciplemaking. (See figure 9-1.) Comparing the Christian life to a trip around the bases on a ball diamond, he illustrates the importance of a disciple's involvement in two spheres of life—church and community. Within the church, the disciple grows in commitment to Christ through worship, nurture, stewardship, and service. But discipleship is incomplete without the involvement of winning new disciples through friendship, witness, the challenge to commitment, and incorporation into the body of Christ, the church. Nikkel insists that Christians must not simply run around the

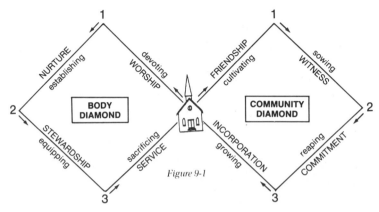

Figure 9-1

bases on the diamond, but must move into the community diamond. Disciples often get stuck at first base on either diamond, resulting in ineffective disciples and/or disciplemakers.

When persons become Christians today, they often say they have "made a decision for Christ." Especially at evangelistic campaigns, it is a common practice to count the number of *decisions* made for Christ. The book of Acts uses different language, referring to believers as *disciples*. In more than two dozen references to disciples in the book of Acts, not one refers exclusively to the twelve disciples. Indeed, every believer is a disciple of Christ.

If disciples faithfully disciple others, who in turn disciple others, the numbers grow amazingly. If one person would win someone to Christ, and disciple him or her for six months, and both would disciple another in the next six months, there would be eight persons at the end of one and one-half years. If this chain of progress were to continue unbroken, after fifteen years there would be 2,147,483,648 discipled persons. Of course, it is hard to imagine such a chain of discipleship which would remain unbroken. But if we are merely content to teach facts or ideas and to muse over gained followers, the amount of disciples will increase very slowly, if at all. Christ calls disciples to make disciples.

For Review, Study, and Discussion

1. How did Paul train leaders?

2. What is the difference between teaching and training? How do they relate to each other?

3. Reflect on the principle of multiplication by disciplemaking. How have parachurch groups used this principle to their advantage? How is your church using this principle?

4. Why did Jesus concentrate on training only twelve men when the needs were so great? What lesson might the church learn from this example?

5. Reflect on the training relationship between Paul and Timothy. Can you cite examples of such relationships in your church?

6. Why is it necessary to teach new converts the importance of discipleship?

Action Challenge

1. Make a list of the ideas, skills, or disciplines you would like new disciples to learn in your church. List them below the examples which have been supplied for you.

IDEAS	SKILLS	DISCIPLINE
God's love	Witnessing	Prayer
Forgiveness		

2. Name several persons in your fellowship or community who might be receptive to a discipleship challenge from you. Ask God to show you whom you should challenge in this way.

3. Outline an action plan for helping a person to become a true disciple of Jesus.

For Further Help

Training Faithful Men, produced by the Institute in Basic Youth Conflicts, Box 1, Oak Brook, Ill. This is an audio seminar with two cassettes by Rev. Dennis Kizziar. It also contains a workbook to be used by a potential disciple and a resource manual for the discipler.

Disciple, by Juan Carlos Ortiz, Creation House, Carol Stream, Ill. This little book outlines in an entertaining way the importance of being a disciple, rather than just a Christian.

Disciples Are Made, Not Born, by Walter A. Henrichsen, Victor Books, P.O. Box 1825, Wheaton, Ill. Henrichsen is deputy director for the Navigators of the Pacific area. This book outlines many of the methods used by the Navigators.

Improving Your Serve, by Charles R. Swindoll, Word Books, Waco, Tex., 1981. Practical, biblical spirituality.

Chapter 10

Leadership and Accountability

The bombing of Pearl Harbor marked a distinct change in perceptions of leadership. In the aftermath of the war which followed, the Japanese emperor declared that he was not divine. In the United States, confidence in governmental leadership was undermined because leaders were unprepared for the Pearl Harbor attack. In Europe, the rise of Hitler had a similar impact. Just before mid-century, confidence in leadership was shaken. Ever since World War II, strong leadership frightens us.

Skepticism and even fear of leadership affect not only the political arena—they also significantly influence the attitudes of Christians toward leaders in the church. The same dismay and skepticism with which people and society perceive their leaders is also reflected in the church. Many Christian communities resist decisive leadership.

Strategies for Leadership

Consequently, a crisis of leadership exists in the church as well as in society. Within the secular arena this crisis has stimulated a new interest in leadership. In recent years a number of books have been written. Two outstanding ones are *Servant Leadership*, by Robert Greenleaf, and *Leaders*, by Warren Bennis and Burt Nanus. These authors apply the tools of sociology and psychology to identify the qualities of effective leadership.

There is a distinction between managerial gifts and leadership gifts. Managers, says Bennis, "do things right, but leaders do the right thing." This is to say that managers work at organizing resources, whereas leaders attract resources to a vision.

Bennis and Nanus identify four basic strategies employed by effective leaders.

1. *Good leaders are persons with a focused vision* that attracts the attention and the commitment of others. They acquire this vision through the art of careful listening. They are able to distill what they have heard and to focus direction with clarity.

2. *Effective leaders position themselves within the tradition, history, and social patterns of the group* in which they are functioning. In this way they establish trust. Good leaders never speak disrespectfully of the people with whom they work. Instead, they establish trust by affirming them, and functioning with constancy and reliability.

3. *Effective leaders communicate their vision meaningfully.* Good communication grabs people. People are led to understand the vision through clear and engaging communication.

4. *Good leaders deploy themselves so as to empower others.* They must become a servant of those whom they are leading. As they deploy themselves, those who have caught the vision begin to carry the vision energetically. It may well be that people may even forget who first communicated the vision to them. This is to say that servant leaders release astonishing amounts of resources and energy.

Bennis and Nanus affirm that the overall goal of effective leadership is empowerment. This is to say that the organizations and the persons surrounding the leader are to be empowered for work. All persons must develop their gifts to the fullest so the vision may be accomplished. Rather than engaging in power plays, the overall goal is the empowerment of people for the task. People become excited about helping to bring about something great and wonderful.

Apostolic Leadership
Acts 6:1-7; 14:21-23; 15:1-2

The qualities of leadership identified by Bennis and Nanus are also described in the book of Acts. The apostolic leaders of the church had a clear and focused vision which they received by listening to the Lord Jesus Christ, the Holy Spirit, the Scriptures, the church, and also by being tuned in to the world in which they lived. Each sermon recorded in the book of Acts reveals a keen awareness of the worldview and perceptions of the audience. These apostolic leaders were good listeners and they developed a *focused vision*.

The *apostles* positioned themselves within the mainstream of Jewish life and thought. In fact, the Christian movement began in Jerusalem, and the temple courts were the early preaching centers.

The first Christian leaders also *communicated* the vision with boldness and clarity, and many were gripped by the reality of Jesus. Soon the Christian movement had extended far beyond the Jerusalem gathering, and new congregations were developing in Samaria, Damascus, and Antioch. The Word of God grew mightily, we read. These new Christians were *empowered* by the reality which gripped the apostles.

These apostolic leaders knew how to share responsibility—to empower others with leadership roles. At one point the Greek-speaking Jewish widows in Jerusalem complained that they were being neglected by the compassion ministry of the church. This ministry apparently included the distribution of food and clothing. So the apostles took immediate steps to empower persons with the authority to lead in this ministry. Seven men were chosen to minister to the disadvantaged widows in the Jerusalem church.

This act of sharing responsibility shows three dimensions of leaders empowering others for ministry.

First, sharing responsibilities helps people feel ownership in the ministry. In this case, the apostles shared responsibility with seven men. The names of those chosen suggest they were members of the Greek Jewish community in Jerusalem. This is to say that when leadership was shared, specific steps were taken to include those who felt like outsiders. In the sharing of leadership, power and authority were also shared to help those who felt powerless begin to experience the affirmation of inclusion in the larger community. The Greek-speaking Jewish Christians were now included in the leadership circle.

Second, the Greek-speaking Jews experienced affirmation and empowerment to work at their own problems in fellowship with the larger church. When the apostles and the church commissioned the seven persons, they were actually affirming the Greek-speaking Jews. This affirmation empowered them marvelously. In fact, these leaders were so excited by this affirmation, that one of them, Stephen, shared the good news of Jesus so enthusiastically that he angered many of the nonbelieving Jews, and he was stoned to death. Before long, Philip proclaimed the gospel in Samaria and helped plant new churches. Then, by the leading of the Holy Spirit, he was taken into the wilderness of Gaza, where he met an Ethiopian eunuch who was traveling from Jerusalem to his home along the Nile Valley of Africa. Philip led this man to faith in Christ, baptized him in a pool of water along the road, and sent him rejoicing on his way to Africa.

The Ethiopian also experienced empowerment through the baptismal affirmation of his faith. According to tradition, his name was Judich. The third-century Christian historian, Euse-bius, reports that he preached the gospel among his people along the Nile River, led many to Christ, and planted many churches.

By entrusting the Greek-speaking Jews with the authority to work at their problems in fellowship with the larger church, an empowerment phenomenon took place which spread far beyond Jerusalem, up to a thousand miles south among desert people of the Nile Valley.

Third, the apostles recognized different leadership roles. As the spiritual leaders of the church, the apostles needed to devote their time to praying and teaching. That was their primary ministry. On the other hand, the seven were given the primary responsibility of collecting funds, purchasing goods, and distributing these goods in a way which would keep peace and harmony in the church. They were commissioned with a ministry of administration, finance, and compassion. The apostles and the seven had different roles in the church.

Pastors and Deacons

Sharing leadership responsibility is always important when a new church is planted. This is partly true because all congregations need both spiritual and managerial leadership. These two functions may be described as the pastoral and deacon ministries of church administration. At first the church planter might need to function in both of these roles. However, if there is a team of persons involved in the church planting effort, it is often wise to differentiate these two roles within the team even before the church is planted. Someone in the team should be recognized as the apostle or pastor whose primary role is to give spiritual leadership to the team. That person needs to focus energies in prayer, teaching the Word, and giving overall spiritual guidance to the group. Another person should be identified to give primary leadership to the administrative functions of the church.

If these gifts and roles are not present in the initial church planting team, then they need to be identified early in the life of the new congregation. In a new church planting, there is often tension between the need to begin to share responsibility and the equally important caution against giving too much responsibility to immature Christians too soon. The danger is that they may become proud or that their possible instability may bring insecurity into the new congregation. The apostle Paul appointed elders in the new congregations he planted rather quickly. The process of leadership development and appointment never took Paul more than three years, and often much less time. Yet he later warns his assistant overseer, Timothy, against ordaining a "recent convert" (1 Timothy 3:6). There are dangers both in moving too quickly and in undue caution. Prayer, counsel with others, and the leading of the Holy Spirit reveal how to move forward in developing the leadership cluster in the new congregation.

As the church grows, the pastor or apostle will need to identify elders who will be his or her pastoral partners. These elders need to be persons filled with the Spirit, people of integrity, people of the Word, and people who share the focused vision of the developing congregation. They must be committed to prayer and they need to have pastoral sensitivity. The church planter/pastor will meet with these people regularly for prayer, fasting, and spiritual discernment in relationship to the overall leadership of the congregation. Occasionally, the pastoral team will call the whole congregation to times of prayer, fasting, and working on the focus of goals and ministries of the fellowship. These spiritual leaders need to be excellent listeners. It is only as they listen to the Holy Spirit, the Scriptures, and to the congregation that their ministry can be authentic and focused.

While the apostolic or pastoral leadership of the congregation forms, the deacon or administrative level of leadership also needs to develop. These are persons with Spirit-directed service and administrative gifts. These persons will have responsibilities similar to those which the "seven" carried in the early church. In many congregations, these persons form the board of deacons or become the church cabinet. The congregational administrators need to function under the overall spiritual leadership of the apostle/pastor and elders.

Overseers or Bishops

The early apostolic church developed a third form of leadership which complemented the leadership of the local congregation. These persons functioned as apostolic overseers. James and Peter seem to have fulfilled this role with congregations in the Jerusalem area. Paul functioned with obvious spiritual authority among the churches he had planted.

Paul's leadership ministry in newly planted congregations reveals an authority which is especially helpful for new congregations. The ministry of overseer, bishop, or area superintendent for a cluster of congregations provides stability and encouragement. Since new congregations are often fragile, this is important. Overseers should be persons of spiritual maturity and wisdom who are intimately acquainted with the church. They should be persons who can counsel the church in times of crisis. The bishop or overseer assists the church in matters concerning the selection and the appointment of leadership. Paul served that function effectively among the churches he planted. Later, Titus also carried responsibility for many churches. The apostle John replaced Paul in Asia Minor as overseer, and he served for many years as an effective bishop within this region. The apostolic church carefully provided spiritual oversight for the clusters of precious churches which the evangels planted.

In order for young churches to thrive, it is usually wise to cluster new congregations together. Paul did not plant just one church in Asia Minor, he planted a cluster of congregations. The same pattern was followed in Macedonia and the Greek

Peninsula. In each case, Paul trained a younger man to become overseer of these clusters of congregations after he left. Titus and Timothy worked together with Paul as associate overseers of the two clusters of churches. Paul and the churches recognized in these men the gift of the Holy Spirit for apostolic leadership. They encouraged that gift, thereby empowering Titus and Timothy for the ministry of being an overseer.

We have identified three dimensions of leadership which were developed as the early church became involved in church planting.

1. Apostolic leaders, most of whom were church planters in their own right, also became overseers of clusters of congregations.

2. Pastoral leaders and elders of new congregations provided the spiritual, pastoral, and teaching ministries of the congregation.

3. Administrators were called to handle finances and ministries of compassion.

Empowerment for Ministry

Ephesians 4:10-13

The purpose of all the leadership functions in the church is to empower every congregational member for ministry. Every new believer in the congregation needs to be equipped and released for ministry. All the gifts of all God's people need to be encouraged and nurtured. This is the ministry of the pastors and elders—spiritual leadership which empowers all for ministry, both new and experienced believers.

Several times in the New Testament, we read that prayer and fasting preceded the selection of leaders. In fact, Jesus spent an entire night in prayer before he called twelve men to become his apostles. In the book of Acts, the same theme recurs. Apparently whenever the apostles and the church needed to take the momentous step of calling leaders, they spent time in prayer and fasting. Leadership selection is a spiritual exercise in which the voice of the Holy Spirit must be heard, or we labor in vain.

Accountability

There is one more aspect of leadership and accountability which must be noted. When the crisis concerning circumcision developed in the church in Antioch, there seemed to be little debate as to where they should go for counsel. A group of the Antioch Christians traveled to Jerusalem for a conference which brought together widely diverse leadership to address the issue and to come to a conclusion. That conference reveals a deep commitment to mutual accountability, even across different cultural and theological perspectives. There was no indication in the early church of any affirmation of an independent spirit. The "cross" and independence just don't belong together. Therefore, as a new community in Christ, they needed to meet with each other in mutual accountability to find the way through the issue at hand.

This principle of accountability, applied today, means that both younger churches and established churches need to find an arena in which they can meet one another as brothers and sisters in Christ. In this way they can reveal to the world that independence is not the mind of Christ. The younger and older churches must find the way together. That is the biblical pattern.

Today the church is probably present in every country in the world. Accountability also has international implications. Just as the Greek and the Hebrew churches in the Acts sought fellowship and accountability with one another, so churches of different languages and cultures today need to seek for ways to learn from each other. As the biblical Christians of Asia, Africa, and Europe found ways to work together in the partnership of the gospel, so also the Christians from the continents, nations, and races of our modern world need consciously to seek for partnership and accountability with one another. Often international denominational relationships are especially helpful in making possible mutual accountability worldwide. Without that international networking, a local congregation can become lonely, or even become seduced by nationalism or cultural relativism. Independence often breeds heresy, for without the counsel of others who also love Christ, we can easily miss the way.

A fundamental way of expressing accountability is to become "servant leaders." Paul writing to the Philippians says, "Your attitude should be the same as that of Christ Jesus, who . . . made himself nothing, taking the very nature of a servant" (Phil. 2:5, 7). When the gospel first came to Uganda over a century ago, some of the chiefs were astonished to learn that Jesus, the Son of God, had washed his disciples' feet. To express this servant spirit of Jesus some of their great chiefs went into the fields to dig in the gardens alongside their servants! Leadership the Jesus way never seeks power. It is not egotistical or authoritarian, or arrogant. Christ-like leadership seeks to minister, serve, and encourage. Such leaders give and receive counsel, for they seek accountability.

Who Is in Charge?

Matthew 16:13-20
It is urgent that every newly planted congregation have clearly defined leadership. Jesus himself made sure of this before his crucifixion. He asked the disciples, "Who do you say I am?"

It was Peter who spoke out on behalf of the others, "You are Christ, the Son of the living God."

Jesus affirmed that confession enthusiastically, and went on to say that on that confession, he would build the church. He expanded, pointing out that the church which is founded on Jesus Christ has authority. He elaborated on the nature of that authority—forgiveness of sins and binding and loosing.

In this passage he also seems to identify Peter as the leader of the group. It is interesting that on the day of Pentecost it was Peter who stepped forward and gave leadership to the other apostles. While he preached on Pentecost day, the other eleven stood with him, supporting what he was saying and affirming his leadership and his preaching ministry. Jesus not only called twelve men to be the apostles of the first church; he also showed that he desired Peter to give overall leadership to the group. Thus, after Jesus ascended to heaven, there was no need for further debate as to whom should give leadership to the group. This had already been clarified by Jesus before his ascension.

In a similar way, it is urgent that leadership responsibilities be clearly identified and defined in every church planting. Who is in charge? That person is first among equals. The person who is in charge is the pastor/church planter, but he or she cannot do the job alone. Elders and deacons need to be identified early in the development of the church to enable the ministry to proceed.

Acts 14:21-23

Paul and Barnabas modeled this concern for clarity in leadership during their first church planting journey into Asia Minor. They planted a cluster of congregations in the Anatola Peninsula in the heartland of present-day Turkey. Then on their way home, they returned to each one of these churches and appointed elders. These apostolic church planters did not neglect the important ministry of calling, identifying, and empowering leaders in each of the precious new congregations the Holy Spirit was creating. Paul never left his congregations with a lack of clarity as to whom was in charge.

Leaders and Models

Philippians 3:13-17; 4:4-9

Paul acted so humbly. Yet he surprised the Philippian church by encouraging them to follow him in every way. How could he say something so astonishing? It was because Paul was aware that the Lord Jesus Christ was being revealed in his life. It was also an admission that he, as the planter of the church of Philippi, had left an imprint on the life and ministry of that congregation. Paul came to Philippi with a team made up of Luke, Silas, and Timothy. Nevertheless, as the leader, his image had been imprinted on that congregation. He was concerned that this image be the image of Christ.

It is wise for the church planter to move with a team like Paul did. This helps the new congregation to see Christ revealed through personalities other than just that of the church planter. For this reason, it is also wise to invite visiting speakers. This helps to provide theological balance in the new congregation.

A modern, inner-city church planter whose ministry has been blessed with exceptional fruitfulness tells his congregation, "Jesus Christ lives in me. I have nothing to hide. You can walk with me through the whole day and you will see that in all I do and say, Jesus Christ is central. Only my wife and I in our bedroom are off limits to your scrutiny. I am no different in public than I am in private. I have no secrets. Jesus is the center of my life. Follow me as I follow Christ!"

A congregation can follow such a leader with joy and confidence. Each church planter needs to walk with Jesus Christ with transparency and commitment. Church planters need to confess before their family, their acquaintances, their church, and their community: "Follow me as I follow Christ!" Many people have never met a born-again Christian. They will first perceive the revelation of Jesus in the church planter, in the team, and in the congregation which the Holy Spirit is developing.

Paul enjoyed being a church planter. His letter to the Philippians is overflowing with joy. What a blessing of grace and privilege it is to be called and empowered for ministry in the church! Paul proclaims: "I will say it again: Rejoice!" People will not follow a morose, pessimistic, or sad person.

Although sobriety is an appropriate pastoral leadership quality, the qualities of joy, hope, vision, and a touch of humor are necessary qualities. A church planter needs to avoid tendencies toward discouragement. Although realism is needed, the church planter Paul, writing from prison, exhorts: "Finally, brothers, whatever is true, whatever is noble, whatever is right, whatever is pure, whatever is lovely, whatever is admirable—if anything is excellent or praiseworthy—think about such things" (Philippians 4:8).

Basic Principles

We have identified five forms of leadership and accountability which are essential for new congregations. There are also ministries which we have not highlighted such as prophet, evangelist, or miracle worker. Our intention here is to highlight roles which pertain particularly to the organization, leadership, and oversight of a congregation. We have described:

1. *The pastor and elders*, who provide the pastoral, prayer, spiritual and teaching ministry, and leadership within the congregation.

2. *The deacons or administrators*, who provide the financial, compassion-oriented, and administrative leadership within the congregation.

3. *The overseer* of a cluster of congregations, who is available for counsel and guidance, and who represents the involvement of the local congregation in the church elsewhere.

4. *The apostle*, who is recognized as a person whom God has anointed with vision, leadership, and authority. Often overseers are apostles, but not necessarily so.

5. *The conference of churches* which can come together for mutual accountability and encouragement.

We have also looked at several biblical principles of leadership, identification, and function:

1. Leadership must focus vision.
2. Leadership must empower others for ministry. Responsibilities must be shared.
3. Leadership must be clearly identified and authentic.
4. Leaders need to be accountable to the congregation and to one another.
5. Leaders should model Jesus Christ.
6. Leaders should rejoice in the gift of grace which has blessed them with the privilege of ministry!

Avoiding Burnout

Ministering joyously and concentrating on the positive help to avoid burnout. We are not aware of any New Testament leaders who experienced so-called burnout, although John Mark did turn back from the work on one occasion. The qualities of joy and a positive attitude which Paul describes in his letter to the Philippians are significant insulation against burnout.

The veteran church planter Paul describes several other basic principles in the Philippian letter which, if observed, will assure that the church planter will enjoy his ministry and protect against burnout. The first three principles are specifically described in the Philippian letter.

1. Don't take yourself or the ministry too seriously. With a twinkle in his eye, to be sure, Paul refers to his personal qualities as garbage (3:7). Even the church was the Lord's and so he was confident that the Lord would bring to "completion" the work he had begun (1:18).

2. Focus on a clear goal. For Paul the goal was to know Christ and to be a faithful minister of the gospel. Keep a clear focus. Learn to know and love Christ. Draw on his strength (3:12-14).

3. Cultivate intimate, supportive relationships with a few people who share the vision. Usually, this intimate support group should not be more than a dozen people. They do not

need to be geographically present, but regular, supportive contact and prayer is essential. It was a tremendous encouragement to receive a letter, a visit, and gifts through the loving concern of the Philippian church when Paul was in prison. Keep in touch with the accountability and support cluster.

4. Maintain good emotional, physical, and spiritual health habits. Disciplined Bible reading, prayer times, and periods for reflection, solitude, and fasting are essential. Enjoy at least one hobby. Get ample recreation. Make family fun time a priority. Keep physically fit: avoid becoming overweight and eat three times daily. Avoid snacks, avoid smoking, alcohol, and drugs. Get regular aerobic exercise and sleep seven hours a night. Take occasional vacations and schedule regular weekly times for rest. Ambassadors of the Lord Jesus Christ should attempt to maintain the mental, spiritual, and physical stamina worthy of their calling as church planters.

5. Married church planters should treasure and cultivate their family relationships. A joyous family is a marvelous asset in church planting. The first ministry responsibility of a married church planter is his or her family. The family can provide much encouragement and support when spouse and children affirm and encourage the vision.

Our observation is that persons who abide by these five principles, undergirded by a joyous and positive spirit, experience resource and ample strength for continued ministry.

Four Kinds of Leaders

Carl F. George of the Charles E. Fuller Institute of Evangelism and Church Growth has helpful insights in relation to leadership style. In a seminar entitled "How to Plant a Church," he shared insights from the business world which also apply in the church planting situation.

Just as businesses grow and decline through stages, churches also experience stages of growth, each calling for a different style of leadership. In the first stage, a *catalyzer* is needed. This kind of person can start a group from scratch, attracting people and other resources. However, such a person becomes frustrated when the size of the group begins to require more and more time and energy for organizational maintenance. As the group matures, catalyzers may drop out of the scene because of frustration, or recruit a teammate with a different mentality to do the work. In business, these persons are valued and compensated highly as entrepreneurs.

A second kind of person may be labeled as an *organizer*. Persons with this skill can take a jumble of pieces and design an orderly organization, making the maximum use of resources. However, they tend to lose a challenge when the original disorder is under control. As organizers mature, they may opt for the benefits of an operator-style management. In business, organizers often advance by changing jobs. In so doing, they often follow up on the work of entrepreneurs.

Catalyzers and organizers are rare. Often, it takes one of these two kinds of persons in order to get a church started. The majority of persons who choose to pursue pastoral ministry do not have the energy or interest in doing the work of starting a new group. Church planters are a precious gift.

A third type of person may be called an *operator*. This kind of person can keep an organization going as long as the main assumptions and approaches to ministry are not changed. However, if there is undue change, or if disorder becomes apparent, this type of person becomes frustrated. As these people mature, they forget how growth occurs and they can easily be defensive in the presence of growth-oriented people. In most congregations, this type becomes a majority.

In most organizations, operators gain control of the system. If they do not learn about the value of catalyzers and organizers, operators will overvalue themselves to the point of discrediting and criticizing the types who precede them. When such attitudes prevail, catalyzers and organizers may exit to build new parachurch organizations or plant other churches.

A fourth kind of person could be named a *redeveloper*. This kind of person tends to bring together some of the strengths of the other three types and can rebuild an organization that has begun to decline. This kind of worker may be called upon to help redevelop a church which has lost its vision or has experienced a lack of growth for many years.

It is valuable to have more than one of these four types of persons in a church planting team. By working together in harmony, each person's temperament can bring what is needed to the church growth task. In the early stages of ministry, a catalyzer can help to gather a group quickly. Another member of the team with organizational ability can help to organize groups and tasks so the work of the church can continue efficiently. Yet another team member with operator tendencies can provide the long-term commitments and "stick-to-itiveness" which is needed to keep a ministry going. These differences of temperament will undoubtedly create tensions, but this is to be expected. By working through these conflicts, each team member can be strengthened in his or her own commitment to the Lord and to the rest of the team.

There are many other ways to work at "categorizing" personalities and leadership styles. The most important thing to consider when "constructing a team" is to be sensitive to the ways in which each personality, temperament, style, and theological convictions will meld with others on the team.

For Review, Study, and Discussion

1. Think of persons you know, and classify them according to their style as Catalyzer, Organizer, Operator, or Redeveloper.

2. Review Bennis and Nanus's four strategies for good leadership. Are these strategies working in the life of a leader you know?

3. Ponder the idea of empowerment. How did the apostles empower others for ministry?

4. Think about the five levels of leadership and accountability explained in this chapter. How does this suggested structure compare or contrast with the leadership approach of your church?

5. Reflect on the role of a bishop or overseer in the church. How might the task of church planting be facilitated by such a person?

6. Review the four kinds of leadership personalities as outlined by Carl George. Which one of the categories best describes your pastor?

Action Challenge

Interview a bishop, overseer, or area superintendent. Ask this person to outline the importance of such oversight for new churches.

For Further Help

Servant Leadership, by Robert K. Greenleaf, Paulist Press, New York, 1977. In this volume, Greenleaf proposes a "first among equals" model, rather than the traditional hierarchical model common to bureaucracy.

Leaders: The Strategies for Taking Charge, by Warren Bennis and Burt Nanus, Harper and Row, Publishers, New York, 1985. After surveying dozens of successful leaders in many organizations, these two men summarized four characteristics of effective leaders.

Overcoming Missionary Stress, by Marjory F. Foyle, MARC, Europe, 1984. A practical, realistic approach to many stress-prone issues in mission leadership.

Chapter 11

Encouragement and Partnering

No truly Christian congregation will ever be independent. Every congregation is a part of a world family of hundreds of thousands of congregations all over the world. Every congregation needs to find ways to partner with the world fellowship.

During the time of the Vietnam War, a small missionary team was helping to plant a church in a Muslim country in Africa. It was a poor country with a per capita income of about $50 per year. A visitor from Vietnam told the story of the suffering of the church in that country as the war was intensifying. The little African congregation of less than ten members took a special offering and sent a gift of several dollars to the church in Vietnam. What an encouragement that was to the Vietnamese church. And what joy it was for the little congregation in Africa to share in a small way with the suffering of their fellow brothers and sisters in Vietnam!

Sometime later, 8,000 miles from that little African church, another congregation located in one of the world's most affluent regions decided to partner with a small church planting fellowship in Boston, Massachusetts. The latter wanted to become a thriving church in that metropolitan area. Occasional visits took place between leaders in the younger Massachusetts fellowship and the established congregation in Mount Joy, Pennsylvania. The Mount Joy congregation contributed finances to help the new fellowship emerge.

Soon the Boston congregation identified itself as Good Shepherd Christian Fellowship and began a prayer ministry for missionaries in other lands. It took offerings to take the gospel to people who did not know of Christ. At the same time, this congregation also developed a partnership with a Messianic Jewish synagogue known as Ruach Israel. The Jewish congregation of believers in Jesus was encouraged that a Gentile congregation welcomed the opportunity for fellowship and partnership.

These two Boston fellowships then decided to develop a facility together. Since this was to be a costly enterprise, the congregational leadership at Mount Joy committed themselves to vigorous assistance in helping to raise the funds for the new facility. As a part of this commitment to partnership, the Ruach Israel Hebrew choral group visited the Mount Joy area. It gave a program in Hebrew song extolling Jesus as Lord. What a refreshing encouragement that was to the Mount Joy church! Thus, all three of these congregations are being blessed and encouraged by their partnerships, and their fruitfulness multiplied.

The examples above illustrate that faithful congregations need to discover ways to partner with other fellowships in their mutual commitment to mission.

Old and New Congregations Need Each Other
Acts 14:21-28; 15:3-4

The church in Antioch commissioned Paul and Barnabas to plant churches among the Gentiles. They traveled to Cyprus and then on to Asia Minor where they planted at least a half-dozen congregations. They were faithful evangelists and effective church planters.

Nevertheless, planting isolated churches was not the intent of their mission. The congregations in Asia Minor clustered in a general region and the church planters returned to visit each of the new fellowships in order to give them encouragement. Certainly a significant aspect of that encouragement was to report what God had done in other cities. They shared the good news that sister congregations had been planted in adjoining communities. Thus, as elders assumed leadership in each of the new congregations, those elders were aware that they were not alone. They, as leaders, and each congregation which they led, were part of a wider cluster of leaders and congregations. Certainly, communication and visits began between the different congregations, bringing encouragement to the new fellowships.

Older, traditional congregations needed encouragement too. Imagine the joy in Antioch when Paul and Barnabas returned from their first missionary journey and reported what the Lord had been doing among the Gentiles in Asia Minor. We read that they stayed there for many days. For this Gentile church in Antioch, the creation of a whole cluster of sister Gentile churches in Asia Minor was exhilarating. It helped stimulate further interest in evangelizing the areas around Antioch.

Later, Paul and Barnabas traveled up to Jerusalem. On the journey they shared with the churches in Galilee and Samaria the good news of what God was doing among Gentiles. Wherever the believers met together and heard the missionaries recounting the acts of the Holy Spirit among Gentiles, there was great joy. When they arrived in Jerusalem, the leaders there received them with open arms. They joyfully told the whole Jerusalem assembly of leaders what God had been doing among the Gentiles.

The good news impacted the Jerusalem congregation. Later, they experienced a significant theological shift in their understanding of the nature of God's covenant community. The younger churches helped to inform and transform the theology of the traditional church in Jerusalem. In partnership, they found the way to be brothers and sisters in Christ across formidable cultural and national barriers.

Sharing Money
Acts 21:17-19; Romans 15:25-27; 2 Corinthians 8:20-21

Later, Paul visited Jerusalem again. This time he came with a "liberal gift" of money from the Gentile churches in Macedonia and Achaia. This is an example of cross-cultural sharing. Prosperous churches sent money to a less prosperous church so the Christian community could experience "equality." The young Gentile churches sent gifts to the church which was older, traditional, and Jewish. The churches of Europe were sending a gift to the churches of the Middle East—moving resources from one continent to another. This experience of sharing dramatically demonstrates the revolutionary new community—the church which the gospel was forming. Never in traditional pre-Christian society had anything like this ever happened before. The gospel forged a partnership—a miracle of God's grace.

On the surface, the gift from the churches of Macedonia and Achaia was to help brothers and sisters in Jerusalem with their physical needs. There were also deeper partnership commitments in this sharing. The Gentile and Jewish congregations were in danger of drifting apart. As we have mentioned before, there were very significant cultural differences between these two communities of Christian faith. The European Gentile congregations and the Asian Jewish churches had almost nothing in common except their commitment to Jesus Christ. Division and schism were a real possibility.

Paul wanted deeply to maintain the unity of the church so both communities could partner together in the world mission of the gospel. For this reason, this sharing of gifts became exceedingly important to Paul. He prepared for the event many months in advance, writing letters and sending messengers to the churches in Macedonia and Achaia. He encouraged them to give generously.

In the process, they developed a whole theology of giving. He took the gift to Jerusalem personally, even though the Holy Spirit clearly witnessed that he would be imprisoned in Jerusalem. For Paul, preserving the unity and the partnership between congregations was so important that he was ready to accept imprisonment in the quest to maintain that unity. He personally carried the gift to Jerusalem from the Gentile churches of Europe. In that mission, he met imprisonment and eventual transfer from home and friends to Caesar's prison in Rome.

A second theme emerges in this account. Paul clearly wanted to avoid the development of suspicion concerning the sharing of this generous gift with the Jerusalem church. He wrote letters and sent personal messengers to the participating congregations to interpret accurately what the purpose of the gift was and how its recipients would use it. He and a team of brothers traveled personally to Jerusalem to deliver the gift to the church. He took care to avoid any darkness of suspicion. He knew that the church must share resources in a trustworthy and completely open manner. He did not take the gift to Jerusalem alone. Others accompanied him on the trip. He understood the need for mutual accountability.

A third principle of partnership is involved in this story. When one fellowship gives with exceptional generosity, it encourages others also to contribute generously. It is good for congregations to stir one another up to good works such as generous giving. It is right to receive encouragement through the generosity of others.

A fourth principle is that congregations should give generously so "there may be equality." The goal of this kind of giving is a movement toward narrowing the gap between the poor and the wealthy.

For many in North America, the standard of living is now about 400 times higher than that of brothers and sisters living in some third-world countries. For example, a schoolteacher in the United States can probably buy about 30,000 eggs with one month's wages. In Somalia, a teacher can buy about 60 eggs with one month's wages. Another contrast: One hour's wages will fill the gas tank for a teacher in Los Angeles. In Kampala, even two month's wages is hardly enough to do that. Partnership in the gospel means that we learn to live generously so we can move toward greater equality within our sisterhood and brotherhood than the world economic system provides.

Hospitality and Mutuality
Matthew 10:5-15; Luke 10:1-12

Jesus was an example of mutuality in mission. When he sent out his disciples to proclaim the gospel, he commanded them to travel in a manner which would guarantee that they would not be self-sufficient. Why? They were to rely on local hospitality. The people who were receiving the gospel were to have the opportunity to respond with generosity.

This is a basic and significant principle of partnership. It is a generous commitment of a congregation to send one of its leaders equipped for ministry to plant a church in a new community. The sending of the missionary is a sacrificial commitment by the sending congregation. They send out their people because of the love of God which they have experienced as a fellowship.

In turn, the community which receives the missionary, hears the gospel, and responds to that good news also needs to have the opportunity to share resources. They, too, have experienced the love of God. In the initial stages of congregational formation, their "thank you" to God should be a financial commitment to the persons who are bringing the gospel. The new believers need to have the opportunity to provide hospitality, which includes lodging, food, and provision for miscellaneous expenses. Thus they have an immediate opportunity to say "thank you" to God by providing hospitality for the church planter.

It is important that the new believers learn the gift of generosity immediately. Soon they will want to send church planters and financial resources to communities beyond themselves. However, the first result of that spirit of generosity needs to be their immediate response to the apostle who has brought them the gospel.

Thus we see that Jesus' approach to ministry builds the theme of mutuality right into the sharing of the gospel of the kingdom. Modern-day church planting needs to proceed in the same way. It is usually not wise for a church planter to move into a community with all financial needs guaranteed by the sending church. The church planting team should move into a community with a sense of dependence upon the community, as it responds to the gospel. Very early in the church planting ministry, the newly emerging church needs to take full responsibility for the support of the church planter. If the church planter receives an allowance or salary, it should not be for long. The new church should soon provide the support. A church planter should not receive long-term financial assistance from a mission board or sending congregation.

Nevertheless, the partnership principle also implies that the extending congregation(s) and the developing congregation may enter into a partnership which might involve sharing of finances. Perhaps a new congregation cannot provide the full-time support which may be needed for the church planter. In that case, the partnering support of the well-established congregation(s) is useful. In such a partnership, the established church sends finances to the new congregation to enable them to provide adequate support for the church planter. Even this type of financial sharing should seldom be long-term. It is not right for the younger congregation to develop permanent dependence on the established congregation. This is one reason why Jesus did not want his missionaries to go with any money in their pockets. He desired that the new fellowship quickly gain a sense of personal responsibility for their own life and ministry. If the church planter came with abundant funds, the new church might never develop a full sense of congregational responsibility.

These principles of mutuality sometimes need modification in international church partnerships, especially when there is a serious economic gap between the partnering churches. Nevertheless, every model of international mission must operate by the biblical principles of mutuality which fosters forms of partnership which avoid dependence, and which enrich and bless all. Biblical mutuality encourages maturity, self-respect, responsibility, and generosity.

Self-Sacrifice and Responsibility
Acts 20:32-35; Philippians 4:12-19

Paul lived by the themes of mutuality, generosity, and responsibility throughout his church planting mission. He often depended on local hospitality, or worked as a tentmaker to support himself and those who were traveling with him. In this way he demonstrated self-sacrifice and self-reliance. Tentmaking was not a noble occupation in Roman society. The Romans considered such craftsmen second-class citizens. Paul was willing to engage in a vocation considered servile. No wonder the Corinthians or the Galatians had difficulty believing that Paul was really an apostle! How could a tentmaker be an apostle? Yet Paul was ready to stoop to tentmaking in order to demonstrate clearly the gospel principle of self-sacrifice and responsibility.

At the same time, however, Paul was also ready to receive the gifts of God's people. Such gifts freed him from the work of tentmaking and allowed him to give himself fully to the task of evangelism and church planting. He commends the Philippians highly for their generous sacrificial giving to enable him to carry on his mission in Achaia after the Philippian church sent him out. This congregation in Philippi gave even beyond their means and capability so Paul could operate unhindered financially in his missionary vocation. Paul received these gifts with joy, since they enabled him to invest all of his energy in church planting.

Whether Paul received financial assistance or not, he was not about to turn away from his vision, call, or mission. He would have continued planting churches even if the Philippians had not sent him funds. Nevertheless, the gifts which came from this Philippian congregation encouraged Paul and helped him minister with greater fruitfulness.

Partnership

We have described three forms of partnership:

1. Clusters of congregations working cooperatively at raising funds to share with impoverished congregations in another region. This "partnering" underscores the broader nature of the kingdom.

2. A newly developing congregation providing hospitality and resources for the persons who are bringing the gospel to them. This increases "ownership" in the local congregation.

3. A congregation or a cluster of congregations supporting a church planter or a team of church planters in mission through prayers, letters, and finances. This is partnering for mission.

All of these forms of partnership spring from a spirit of sacrificial generosity. Sometimes church planters should earn their own living through manual labor as a sign to the new congregation of the sacrificial nature of gospel ministry. At other times it is better to receive assistance from partnering congregations.

Basic Commitment

In our modern world there are hundreds of thousands of congregations around the globe. The mechanisms of partnership are, therefore, more complex than they were in the days of the apostles. Congregations vary in character nearly as much as do cultures. Nevertheless, the basic principles still apply. Whoever confesses Jesus Christ as Lord and Savior is part of the new community which God has redeemed. All these churches need to express in their actions towards one another the spirit of Christian love and partnership.

A minimal commitment is for all Christians everywhere to commit themselves not to kill one another. That form of Christian partnership would be a tremendous step toward world peace. Paul and the Corinthian church would never have taken up arms against James and the Jerusalem church if Corinth and Jerusalem had gone to war with one another. The Christians would never have participated. The early Christians could not conceive of fighting each other, even if their countries went to war. Should modern Christians love one another any less?

Denominations and Mission Boards

Partnership takes many forms, including sharing resources with one another. Often two congregations will partner together. On an international basis, however, that is usually impractical. This is why a mission board or a church relief and development agency can be helpful. The role of a mission board is to help congregations do collectively what one congregation could not do alone in the partnership of the gospel. Mission boards and relief agencies need to be servants of congregations to help them in their partnership with other congregations in distant places. They can enable evangelistic and missionary ministry in a more effective manner than one congregation alone could do.

Because of the size and diversity of the Christian church today, most congregations find it convenient to work their partnership commitment through a denominational relationship. Denominations are international families of churches in harmony with a common Christian tradition. In a special way they are partners in the cause of the gospel.

We believe that it is wise for a newly planted church to avoid the modern tendency of being independent. The biblical partnership model happens when congregations affiliate with a denomination. It happens whenever a church partners with an international cluster of congregations who flow with a common vision. Young churches should make their denominational affiliation clear right from the beginning. They should not wear themselves out by attempting to express dynamic partnership relationships with all of the different denominational clusters around the world. This would become exhausting and confusing.

We believe it is the wisest course for a new congregation to develop an explicit commitment to a particular denomination or family of churches. This denomination should be in harmony with the theological commitment and tradition of the church planter. In this way, the congregation can soon begin to focus energy in its local, national, and international commitment to partnership with other congregations in the cause of the gospel. Focused partnership is more effective than scattered and diffused partnership commitment. Denominational affiliation helps such focused partnership to happen.

This is not to say that congregations should commit themselves to denominationalism. "Isms" can become evil. We commit ourselves to Christ, not to an "ism." It is wrong for one's denominational commitment to become so important that the congregation does not relate to Christians of other denominations. It represents a serious division in the body of Christ. We dare not permit our denominational commitments to bring schism into the body of Christ. The purpose of a denominational commitment is not division, but rather affirmation of the richness of the tradition and theology of one family of congregations in our world today. It is joyfully to embrace the partnerships which affiliation to that family of faith can provide.

For Review, Study, and Discussion

1. Reflect on the example of partnership between the Mount Joy and Boston congregations. What significance might this interaction have for the life of the three churches?

2. Review the reasons why Paul was so eager to develop partnership between congregations. How might one use his strategy to good advantage in a church planting situation today?

3. Consider the importance of hospitality in a church planting situation. How might a church planter learn to give and receive hospitality?

4. Think about the importance of self-sacrifice in church leadership. How did Paul model this concept?

5. Study the three forms of partnership explained in this chapter. In what ways is your church participating in one or more of these ways?

6. What might be the advantages and disadvantages of denominational affiliation? What steps can one take to prevent a movement toward unhealthy denominationalism?

7. What are the dangers of independence?

Action Challenge

1. Interview the person in your congregation charged with the task of disbursing the funds. What percent of congregational giving does the congregation spend on itself? What percent goes toward its partnership with other churches or individuals in mission or relief work?

2. Interview a pastor or church leader of an "independent" church. What forms of partnership does this church experience? What might be the advantages or disadvantages of being an "independent" church?

3. Think of ways in which your church could develop new ways of partnering in the gospel. Think of mission giving, hospitality, prayer commitments, church planting, and so forth.

For Further Help

Administrative Guidelines for Church Planting, published by Eastern Mennonite Board of Missions, Oak Lane and Brandt Blvd., Salunga, Pa. A simple, practical presentation of how one group provides administration and support for church planting in the United States.

Pilgrimage in Mission, by Donald R. Jacobs, Herald Press, Scottdale, Pa., 1983. A biblical theology and practical approach to issues in modern mission.

Chapter 12

Facilities
and Finances

It happened in an elevator in Washington, D.C. It was a memorable prayer meeting for David. Three of us had just completed an agreement in a lawyer's office to purchase a church building for a new congregation in the capital city of the United States. As we stepped into the elevator, we three men drew into a tight circle and gave thanks to the Lord. Within seconds the elevator had stopped at the ground floor. One person dashed for an airplane, another brother headed for the train station, and a third to another Washington appointment.

We three who gathered in that elevator were the church, the body of Christ. In those few seconds we had gathered in Jesus' name and confessed his lordship with thankfulness. As soon as the elevator door opened, we scattered in three different directions, but we knew that we were the church scattering in ministry.

The Church Building

Acts 2:46; 12:12-14; 16:11-15

Whenever we consider a facility for the church, we always need to remember that a building or a place is not the church of Jesus Christ. It is the people who gather in Jesus' name who are the church. Thus it was that in the Washington elevator, the church had formed. The building we had agreed to purchase was not church, but we three were church. Wherever two or more gather in Jesus' name, that is the church. That gathering can take place anywhere at anytime, and it is always the church. Facilities or instruments of worship are never essential to the formation of the church.

However, facilities can be useful tools for the church to use in its life and ministry. It would be quite uncomfortable for people to gather in Jesus' name under a leafless cherry tree in the wintertime in Washington. A heated meeting place is preferable. Facilities are useful because a church needs a place to meet.

In the New Testament there was diversity and creativity in the selection of meeting places. During the first month after the formation of the church in Jerusalem, Christians met in large gatherings in the temple area. This was the place where the Jewish people had gathered to worship God for centuries. Since the early church experienced the fulfillment of God's promises to Israel, they felt it completely natural to worship the Lord Jesus Christ together in the temple area. Later on, as the temple leadership became increasingly opposed to the Christian movement, it became impossible for the Christians to meet in the temple area for their celebrations of joy.

Yet the Christians were not dismayed by exclusion from the temple. Right from the beginning they had discovered an alternate place for worship which was in complete harmony with the nature of the church. This was the family living room. Right from the birth of the church, the believers began to gather together in homes throughout Jerusalem. The gathering at the temple seemed to have been mostly for mass gatherings for celebration and teaching. But much of the life of the early church was carried on in the homes of the believers. This model was extended wherever the church was planted in the countries of Africa, Asia, and Europe. It is not surprising, therefore, that several decades later when Paul wrote to Philemon, he saluted, "The church that meets in your house" (Philemon 1:2).

Christians met in many kinds of locations. The church at Philippi began along the shore of a river. Although Philippi was a city with many different facilities which could have been used for the Christians to gather, Paul and his team discovered that the most fruitful place to meet people was at the riverside. So that is where the church began. Soon the congregation seems to have moved into the home of Lydia. Doubtlessly, other house churches were formed as well, but the first congregation met by the river.

When possible, Christians met in the Jewish synagogue. In fact, many years later when Christians began to construct meetinghouses for their worship, the architecture of those so-called "church buildings" was quite similar to that of the synagogue. The synagogues had a number of advantages for Christian meetings.

1. *The synagogue was quite large* and could accommodate more people than was usually true of a house.

2. *The facility was always available.* When a congregation had access to a home, it had to meet at times convenient to the family, and of course the homeowners needed to clean up any living-room clutter before every church meeting. In contrast to this, it was pleasantly convenient to have a place specifically designated for Christian gatherings.

3. *The synagogue had the articles which were used in the worship experience.* For example, the Scriptures were there. The only Bible of early Christians was the Old Testament. Since these scrolls were expensive, handwritten Scriptures, they

were stored safely in the synagogue and were accessible to the worshipers.

As the Christian congregation developed, the Jewish leaders eventually required them to leave the synagogue. Sometimes this break between the church and the synagogue was painful and even violent. When they could no longer worship in the synagogue, Christians often formed a number of smaller gatherings in their private homes, as the first Christians had done in Jerusalem. The movement from the synagogue to private homes is vividly described in the planting of the church in Corinth.

Sometimes the Christians were able to find another building which provided many of the desirable qualities of the synagogue for their meetings. This was the pattern in Ephesus, where Paul found a hall which he used for two years as a base for the development of congregations throughout the region.

Some scholars believe that this facility was available because they used it in the heat of the day, while the Greeks who used it at other times were resting in a cooler spot. In that event, they would have had restricted access to the building. Certainly the hall did not substitute for the house churches which were forming in the area, but it did provide a larger place for Christians to meet than would have been possible in most of their small homes.

It might be that the church in the Ephesus metropolitan area developed a worship rhythm. Probably cell group house churches multiplied throughout the city. The small fellowship groups engaged in confession, prayer, singing, the study of Scriptures, and the breaking of bread together. Then there may have been the larger gathering in the hall of Tyrannus, where all the Christians in the area could meet for praise, worship, celebration, and hearing the Word of God proclaimed. The rhythm of small group fellowship and large celebration events is a model which may have developed in Ephesus, and which is being used by many metropolitan churches today.

Versatility

Matthew 5:1; Luke 4:16

Jesus set the pattern for versatility in worship. Sometimes he gathered his disciples together for an open-air church service. He met with two or three for a private hilltop meeting or proclaimed the gospel of the kingdom to as many as 20,000 people in an open-air natural hillside arena by the Sea of Galilee. On other occasions he met in the synagogues, where he was perfectly at home with the simple decor and Scriptures always present. Jesus also met in the temple, where on several occasions he created quite a stir. In the context of the temple he seemed particularly concerned with communicating that the true temple of God is not a building, but rather a people of God who gather in worship and commitment.

In the entire New Testament, there is never any indication that the Christians occupied themselves with collecting funds for developing a center for worship. All fund-raising efforts were devoted toward ministries—never toward an investment in a facility. This is particularly surprising when one considers that the other religions of the day invested enormous treasures in the construction and maintenance of sacred places for worship. The temple for the worship of Diana in Ephesus was one of the seven wonders of the ancient world. The Jewish temple in Jerusalem consumed enormous resources in its construction and maintenance. In contrast to this, there is no evidence that the church ever invested a denarius in a building. The church is not a building; it is the people of God!

It is not wrong for a church to invest in developing a facility, if necessary. However, the biblical models clearly reveal that the investment of funds in a building is less important than forming the body of Christ and ministry. The most legitimate investment of church finance is in ministry to the poor and in the extension of the kingdom through evangelism and missionary activity. Putting funds into bricks and timber which have nothing of eternal quality about them is legitimate only as it assists the church in its ministry.

Churches do need places to meet. Sometimes the ministries of the church—providing food for the hungry, or shelter for the homeless, or feeding people spiritual food through the teaching of the Word of God—are best fulfilled when the church has access to its own facility. In that case, the purchase of a structure is right. Whenever that is necessary, however, the facility should be simple and involve a minimal investment of treasures. The stewardship of the gospel requires that the primary commitment of the congregation should be to invest in people, not in buildings.

Facilities are also important because they provide memory for the congregation. Anthropologists refer to this human need as the sacred place. Recently in inner-city Brooklyn, Pastor Vicente Martinez took his friend from the country to see the church building in which he had been nurtured in faith through childhood, youth, and young adulthood. Vicente was ecstatic with joy as he showed the spot he was sitting at when he first committed his life to Christ. Reverently, he showed his friend the pulpit and described the preachers who had ministered the Word from that place. The Sunday school rooms, the basement fellowship hall with the flooring Vicente had helped to lay, all were precious. Outside the elevated trains clanged, buses and trucks jostled, radios thumped rock from kiosks. Inside, those two men were in sacred retreat drinking in the poignant memory of precious gifts of grace. Indeed, people do need places for retreat, solitude, and memory.

It is wise for a new congregation in need of a place to consider the ethos of the community in which the congregation is located before developing the facility. For example, location is important and will help to determine the kind of people who will be attracted to the new congregation. The kind of facility and aesthetic decor should be an expression of the cultural sensitivities of the community. Although extravagance is never right, simplicity and gentle beauty are always appropriate.

When a congregation must purchase or build a facility, this should not detract from the importance of congregational fellowship and worship in the house church setting. The larger facility should be perceived only as the rallying place and ministry center for the various cell groups meeting in homes throughout the metropolitan area or countryside. The church building should help the rhythm of healthy church life, with meetings in small cell groups in homes on the one hand, and the large celebration event on the other. In this way, the Word of the Lord is proclaimed amidst the full worshiping congregation, consisting of many cell groups which come together from throughout the area to reaffirm their common unity in Jesus Christ.

Financial Caution

When a congregation decides to invest in a building, it should not become overextended financially. It is sad when a church invests so much treasure in a facility that resources are not available for mission and ministry. We also believe that it is not wise for a congregation to borrow funds for the development of a facility which cannot be paid back within ten years. The ministries and the visions of a congregation continue to grow and change. Most churches discover that the excitement of investing in a church building wears off within ten years. A newly emerging vision may be hampered by the burden of paying off a debt invested in a building.

A congregation needs to work carefully to discern whether it is right to invest in a facility. However, if the life and ministry of the congregation is enhanced through the ownership of a building, then it is right for the congregation to take steps of faith toward the goal of owning its own building. The determining question is this: Will this building be a helpful tool for the life and mission of this congregation? It is often helpful for a church to have a place of its own where the members can retreat from the pressure and clamor of life. A facility can become a base for effective ministry, and a sign in the community of the long-term commitment of the new congregation.

Mission and Ministry

Once, in Harlem, New York City, mission board people and the leaders of a small congregation met to talk about the needs within that community. For many years that congregation had been meeting in a renovated storefront which doubled as a Head Start child care facility during the week. It was also a congregation whose members had experienced some dislocation due to apartment fires on the block where the meetinghouse was. Homelessness was a serious problem in that community. Many assumed that the primary need of the congregation was adequate housing, but that was not the case.

All of the people with roots in Harlem said that the first need of the church is a chapel, a sanctuary, a place of retreat from the clamor of the city. They wanted a building people could point to as the place where the church meets. So the congregation committed itself to an ambitious church building project. Indeed, having a place for retreat and mission is sometimes exceedingly important. In that case, the church should take the necessary faith steps.

Consideration of finances is necessary for a building project. In fact, finances are needed to carry out most of the forms of life and ministries in the congregation. It is not surprising that when the apostles first formed the church, one of the immediate expressions of Christian experience was the selling of property and the distribution of goods to the poor within the believing community. Financial sharing and Christian experience belong together. It has always been so in the life and ministry of the church.

Although it may be necessary for a congregation to invest significant treasure in a church building, the primary commitment of treasure must always be in ministry to the poor, and to the extension of the kingdom.

Financial Responsibilities

2 Corinthians 8:1-24; 9:1-15

How should a newly formed congregation handle its finances? Paul commented extensively on this question in his second letter to the Corinthian church, a congregation he had planted during his second missionary journey. Several basic principles are clear in his counsel to this congregation.

1. *Giving is part of the experience of worship.* When a congregation gathers for worship in its regular weekly meeting, an opportunity should be provided to give finances or other forms of wealth for the ministries of the church. This should take place in the midst of the worship experience. It is part of joyous worship.

2. *Giving is an important way of expressing appreciation for the grace of God* as revealed in our Lord Jesus Christ. As Christ became poor for us, so we also lower our standard of living by giving generously through the congregational offering. Giving is a sign that we have been enriched by Christ's poverty and that we desire in turn to enrich others through our acts of sacrificial giving. It is a practical way of expressing appreciation for the grace of God.

3. *Giving should be systematic.* Throughout the week or month, as one receives income through labor, investments, or good fortune, the person should lay aside a portion of the wealth gained for investment in the cause of the kingdom. The giving should be in proportion to the wealth that one has received. It should be the "firstfruit," the best and first that one has received. In firstfruit giving, tithing is often a minimum goal. Most Christians in affluent North America will want to give far beyond the tithe.

4. *It is often good to designate giving.* In this case, Paul asked the Corinthians to designate offerings for their poor brothers and sisters in the church in Jerusalem. Designated giving helps to give the congregation a sense of personal ownership in the ministries of the church. Also by designating

the giving, offering by offering, new congregations learn to know what the various ministries of the church are.

A minimal commitment of any new or established congregation should be the designation of at least one offering per month for mission beyond the church. Perhaps that mission offering should take place the first Sunday of each month, after people have their paychecks, for a healthy new congregation will want to keep world missions right at the center of its vision. Even the mission offering can be designated. For example, one offering per month can go for a church planting effort in a sister community and another offering going for outreach to Muslims in the Middle East.

By designating offerings which relate to the specific ministries of the local congregation, new believers quickly begin to learn the various aspects of congregational life. As the designated offering is shared, the congregation should also engage in prayer for the ministry to which the offering is devoted.

Some congregations have a unified budget, with all offerings going directly into the same fund. This fund is then disbursed according to a previously determined pattern. One of the problems of the unified budget is that it often takes new believers many years to comprehend the full-orbed dimensions of the ministries of the local church.

Furthermore, there is often less "ownership" in various ministries when persons do not have the opportunity of contributing to designated offerings. People are seldom inclined to give sacrificially to a "budget." If a newly planted congregation does decide to go with a budget plan, that church should periodically have a special above-budget joy and celebration offering explicitly devoted to the world mission of the church. Indeed, Paul called upon the Corinthians to give generously above the normal ministries of their church for their brothers and sisters overseas.

5. *The offering must be handled in a way which avoids all*

suspicion. Paul was exceedingly careful in handling the offering and in the end he and several brothers accompanied this gift to Jerusalem. This is exceedingly important in all congregations, and especially so in a newly planted church. Designated offerings *must* always go only for the ministry for which the offering was given.

6. *The churches Paul planted never developed financial dependency on other congregations.* Financial assistance was always short-term. Each congregation developed the resource base needed for its own life and ministry.

Practical Guidelines

Our experience shows that the following commitments will go a long way toward establishing a congregation's finances on firm footing.

1. *At least two persons should collect and count the offering.*

2. *The congregation should see regular reports* of the money received and the way in which it was used.

3. *There should be an annual audit of the accounts of the church* by a person not involved in any way in the receiving or distribution of the offerings.

4. As soon as possible, *the church planter and the congregation should select a person other than the pastor to serve as treasurer* of the congregation. If the church planter is part of a team, another member of the team should serve as treasurer even before the church begins meeting publicly. This should be a member who is not receiving pay from the congregation. It is important that right from the beginning, or as early as possible, anyone who is receiving pay from the congregation be disqualified as treasurer of the church.

5. *Simple but adequate bookkeeping procedures are a must.* The books should always be open for perusal by anyone in the congregation who desires to see them.

6. *A group of persons appointed for that responsibility should make decisions concerning the allocation of funds.* Or,

the congregation could make those decisions together. However, it is sometimes advisable for the pastor or church planter to have access to a small petty cash fund to use at his discretion for persons in his pastoral ministry who need minimal forms of assistance.

7. *Designated offerings should include prayer for the ministries for which the offering will be shared.* A word of information about the ministry often helps to encourage a generous response.

8. *One should be cautious about borrowing funds for facility development or purchase.* Our experience is that it is usually not wise to enter into a mortgage which exceeds ten years. Often church agencies can arrange low-interest loans for new congregations. In the United States, such lending arrangements are sometimes regulated by the Securities Exchange Commission. Yet the red tape is often well worth the effort. Providing low-interest loans or grants for facilities for new churches is often a major help in establishing the new church.

9. *The congregational leaders need to encourage and teach Christian stewardship,* not by constraint, but out of the joy which springs up in the hearts of those touched by the grace of our Lord Jesus Christ. Tithing should be a minimum goal. The experience of sharing the offering each Sunday should be one of joy and celebration. Do not sing songs which depress one's spirit when the offering is collected. Celebration songs are far more appropriate to the joy of giving for the ministries of the church of Jesus Christ.

10. *It is important that the new congregation begin to experience the vision of giving right from the beginning.* When the first Bible study takes place in the living room of the church planter, an offering basket should be present. This is a sign of commitment by that little fellowship, which at that point probably includes persons who are not even committed to the vision and perhaps are not even believers. The offering basket is a sign of faith, a sign of commitment, and a sign of joy that

the grace of our Lord Jesus Christ is present in that little Bible study fellowship.

11. *Often new congregations designate the offering from its first public Sunday morning worship service explicitly for the purpose of sharing the gospel* with people who have not yet heard of our Lord Jesus Christ. That offering should be a joyous thanksgiving that God is creating a new church in this community committed to extending this same gospel everywhere. An offering for unreached people is an appropriate way to reveal to all present the vision of the new congregation to be a church reaching out beyond themselves.

12. *Never develop a long-term dependency situation.* Dependency is spiritually unhealthy.

As we visit new churches, we are often amazed at the diversity of ways in which offerings are received. We do not necessarily recommend all of those approaches, yet they illustrate the cultural diversities in which the church fulfills its giving mission.

In Munich, Germany, a new congregation encourages each person to arrange for automatic monthly computerized transfer of designated funds from their personal checking account into the church account. Computers and banks handle the giving so no time is wasted in passing an offering basket in this efficiency-conscious society.

In Nairobi, Kenya, on special offering days for a new congregation, persons bring their offering forward. Each person's gift is publicly counted and announced. Then there is a special twelve-clap applause by the congregation. If the first round of offering is not enough, they continue to take the offering until they reach their goal.

In Brooklyn, New York, a new fellowship places the names of each person with his or her monthly salaries on a chart in front of the congregation. When one has brought one's tithe for the month, a gold star is affixed on the chart in front of that person's name.

In Hong Kong a congregation passes the offering basket in silence and gentle dignity.

In Accra, Ghana, there is dancing, drums, and song as the worshipers move to the front with their gifts. Goats, chickens, eggs, or milk are given as readily as cash in this Ghanaian church.

In Tegucigalpa, Honduras, there are four kinds of giving in a new congregation. Everyone is expected to tithe. There are also the regular weekly offerings which are always above the tithe. The tithe giving and the offering giving are completely separate forms of giving. Then there is the emergency giving for special needs. Finally, there is the celebration giving on festive occasions when there is a total outpouring of generosity and praise.

A congregation in Boston does not yet have much cash available for anything. These people give their time. They have formed a disaster service, and send volunteers to help when they hear of need, such as a flood in a nearby state.

The patterns of giving in congregations around the world form a beautiful tapestry which fills the heart of God with joy.

For Review, Study, and Discussion

1. Reflect on the use of the word *church*. Often it is used to refer to building facilities. How might this practice affect your concept of the church?

2. Remember that buildings for use exclusively by church groups were almost nonexistent in the first two centuries after Christ. What has changed to make church buildings so prominent today?

3. How might the availability or nonavailability of a worship facility affect the life of a modern-day church group?

4. Review the practical guidelines for financial commitments in a church situation. Do you agree or disagree with these guidelines? Can you think of others?

5. What is your response to the idea that new churches

should develop financial independence as soon as possible? What might be some advantages and disadvantages of such a stance?

Action Challenge

1. Study the financial principles which emerge in Paul's counsel to the church of Corinth. Are these being incorporated into the life of your church?

2. Obtain a financial statement of your congregation's giving in the past year or so. Are you partnering in significant ways with another fellowship? If not, challenge your leadership to develop a vision for such partnership.

For Further Help

Rich Christians in an Age of Hunger, by Ronald J. Sider, InterVarsity Press, Downers Grove, Ill., 1982. A biblical study of Christian stewardship in our global village in which hunger and luxury coexist.

Unleashing the Church, by Frank R. Tillapaugh, Regal Books, 1983. A description of an urban church in dynamic ministry with minimal investments in facilities.

Chapter 13

New Congregations in Mission

About two dozen church planters gathered in the fall of 1984 in the small mountain town of Liberty, Pennsylvania, for fellowship, refreshment, and prayer. They shared stories of the grace of our Lord Jesus Christ and his redemptive power in their communities. Just as Paul and Barnabas, many centuries before, had encouraged the church in Jerusalem by telling of the conversions of Gentiles, so these church planters were encouraged as they shared their stories. They told about men and women who had been born again as the Holy Spirit empowered people to share the gospel faithfully.

As the group prayed and fellowshiped together, their vision began to expand beyond their communities and congregations. The Lord began to reveal a vision for the whole world, and especially for people who had not yet heard the gospel. One person present reminded the church planters that there are still more than 16,000 people groups who have not yet heard enough of Jesus Christ to make an informed decision. The church planters gathered in intercessory prayer and began to cry out to God, "Lord, what would you have us do?"

As they prayed, the Holy Spirit led the group to plan for a new commitment to world missions. At the last session of this church planters conference, a group was called to give leadership to the vision, four women and four men. The Holy Spirit led the group to investigate Peru.

In the months that followed, the vision grew as they began to research the situation in Peru. They learned of a large tribe of several million unreached people in Peru called the Quechua Indians, the descendants of the ancient Incas. Congregations which were only a year old, along with others which had achieved the mature age of six or seven years, began to send in their offerings. Within less than a year, they had received over $20,000 as seed funds toward the outreach effort of sharing the gospel with the people in Peru who had not yet responded to Jesus. The group, now known as the Servants of Love to Peru, have given good leadership to the vision, and a growing number of newly planted congregations are committed to sharing their people and their resources to fulfill this vision from the Lord.

Center of World Mission

Acts 16:13-40; Philippians 4:15-16

These twentieth-century church planters are similar to the first-century church in Philippi. That congregation also experienced the joy of seeing diverse people in their community transformed through the power of the gospel. We know of the conversion of a few of them. Lydia was a wealthy, self-sufficient businesswoman. A demonized slave girl was oppressed and exploited. A jailer, attuned to the violence and oppression of the Roman colonial system, believed. These were the kinds of people who came to salvation through the faithful witness of church planter Paul and the team who was with him.

The church in Philippi also had a vision for mission beyond their city. As the twentieth-century church planters were captured by a vision from the Lord to share the gospel with un-reached people, so the church in Philippi was gripped. The Philippians caught a vision to extend the gospel of the kingdom of God to other cities, regions, and nations. This is why they sent finances to Paul to assist him in his church planting efforts in other cities to the south such as Thessalonica, Berea, Athens, and Corinth. The missionary offerings of the church in Philippi helped to free Paul from financial burdens, thereby enabling him to invest more time in the church planting effort to which God had called him.

Romans 15:25-29

In fact, the new congregation in Philippi later extended their missionary commitment all the way to Rome by sending gifts to Paul, imprisoned in the Imperial City. We know that Paul felt a call from the Lord to take the gospel to Spain, and that he hoped his stay in Rome would be temporary. He saw it as a stepping-stone on his way to the easternmost shores of Europe.

Certainly the Philippians knew of this vision, for Paul had not kept this sense of mission a secret. Perhaps this is one reason why they so eagerly and sacrificially arranged for Epaphroditus to take their generous gift to Paul in the Roman prison. They may have hoped that upon release from prison, he could use this gift toward his travel and maintenance expenses on his mission to Spain. They did not want the mission to be hindered in any way.

The ancient tradition of the church holds that the Roman authorities did release Paul from prison briefly, enabling him to carry the gospel to Spain. Perhaps that gift from the Philippian church enabled that mission to be fulfilled.

Paul was overjoyed by this generous commitment to him and to mission by the Philippian Christians. Although this was a young church, they did not want the joy of mission to be the exclusive possession of so-called "established" congregations. No, they also wanted to be part of the vision and gave so the ministry of the gospel could go forward without delay.

It is that kind of vision which the Spirit of God desires every congregation to enjoy. No matter how young or how small a new church may be, God wants it to be a center for world mission. One does not measure the significance of that center by the quantity of financial or personnel resources which a congregation generates. Rather, one looks at the clear vision, prayer, and sacrificial commitment of that congregation to the world mission of the church.

The Joy of Mission

John 4:34-36

We know that our Lord rejoices when newly planted fellowships reach out with the sacrifice and commitment of the first-century metropolitan church of Philippi, or the twentieth-century church planters retreat in Liberty, Pennsylvania. These kinds of congregations move with the same vision and heartbeat which Jesus himself revealed when he met with the woman of Samaria at the well just outside Sychar. The disciples had gone into town to purchase food, and when they returned to Jesus, they offered lunch. But he turned it down, saying that he had found food to eat which was more satisfying than bread for the stomach. The food he was eating was the joy of seeing a spiritually and morally devastated person transformed by grace. The miracle of a Samaritan woman being made new as she met the Messiah touched Jesus with such joy that food itself had lost its attraction.

Then he turned to his disciples and asked them, "Can't you see?" The world is as a field of grain ready for harvest. Pray that God will send forth laborers into his harvest field.

As Christians, we experience many dimensions of worship and church life. None touches us with greater joy than someone who meets Jesus for the first time, or when a sinner repents and turns to the Lord. It is not hard for us to believe that the angels in heaven sing with joy. We, also, are anointed with indescribable joy. The same is true when the Spirit of God calls laborers from within our congregations to go into the world harvest field to help to bring in the grain before it rots and dies. That is also indescribable joy.

Every Church a Missionary Fellowship
Matthew 4:18-20; 28:18-20

The intention of Jesus is that every congregation experience the joy of evangelism in its normal life together. This is true of so-called "established congregations"; it is also true of newly planted churches. It is no wonder that when Jesus called his first disciples to follow him, his first words to them were, "Follow me. I will make you fishers of men." The discipling church is an evangelistic church. The touchstone of authentic discipleship is the evangelistic vitality of a congregation. New congregations need to concern themselves with leading new believers into a full commitment to Jesus Christ as Lord and Savior.

This includes obedience to the full-orbed ethical teachings of Jesus and the apostolic writers. The test of the disciples' faithfulness is compassion for the lost. That's why Jesus said that disciples who follow him will be fishers of men. They will be evangelists.

Jesus' final words to his disciples before his departure into heaven were a reaffirmation of the truth that those who follow Jesus, share Jesus. In each one of the versions of his farewell words with his disciples, the central theme is the same: You will be witnesses! The vision of Jesus was that of an expanding witness which would move outward from the first Jerusalem congregation. Every faithful congregation is also that kind of world mission center with a missionary vision. It begins in urban Jerusalem, moves into the security of suburban Judea, and reaches out to the dispossessed of Samaria. It culminates in witness to the peoples of the earth who have not yet heard the name of Jesus.

The Miracle of God's Love

John 17; 1 Corinthians 1:11,16

Every congregation needs to confess that the central quality of authentic mission is unity and love. The unity and love expressed in congregational life and ministry stands as the proof that Jesus is Lord and Savior.

Both the Corinthian church and the congregation at Philippi were quite diverse. There was no sociological glue to hold these congregations together. In Philippian society it was unprecedented for a wealthy merchant woman to have intimate fellowship with a slave girl. That just was not done. There were no models in Philippi for that kind of community.

When Paul wrote to the Corinthians, he referred to those of Chloe's household and these of Stephanas'. Modern researchers help us to understand that these households were at opposite ends of the sociological and economic spectrum in Corinthian society. Yet in Christ these two communities were experiencing unity. This was a miracle of grace which astonished the traditional community. It was unprecedented.

The same thing had happened in Antioch, where Jews and Greeks had met each other in Christ. In Antioch, Africans, Asians, and Europeans also came together in this new fellowship.

These new communities of unity and love are replicated wherever the gospel is received. In recent years in Tel Aviv, Israel, a congregation has been created through the mighty working power of the gospel, which brings together Arabs from Muslim background, secularists from Caucasian or Semitic background, and Jews from an Orthodox background. This is a miracle of God's grace in the midst of hate and violence which so characterizes much of the Middle East today. This kind of miracle is the heartbeat of evangelism. It is a revelation of the gospel which can be touched and felt and experienced. These are signs that Jesus is indeed Lord and Savior, and that the gospel is, indeed, the good news that God has acted in the cross to reconcile us to himself and to reconcile enemies with one another.

During the genocidal civil war, which tore at the social fabric of Rwanda in Central Africa during the 1960s, many revivalist Christians refused to fight one another. Many died from beatings they received. As they died, they cried out to their enemies, "We forgive. Because of the Lord Jesus Christ, we forgive you." Others gathered together in schools and churches throughout the countryside. These became islands of reconciliation and peace in the midst of unfathomable hate and destruction. Persons from all of the warring groups who knew Jesus gathered together in these centers of reconciliation. They spent time repenting of anger and hatred, confessing their sins to one another, singing praises to the Lamb of God who brings about reconciliation.

The praise and song which arose from these reconciliation centers was so noteworthy that the warring factions began to nickname them the "praise centers." Amid genocidal war which exalted death and destruction, these Christians became the primary reconcilers in Rwandan society.

Moving Out from the Center

2 Corinthians 5:17-21

The stories of the church as a reconciliation community are precious. They are authentic signs of the kingdom of God present on earth. However, just being a community of peace is not sufficient. Paul reminded the Corinthians, who were committed to being a reconciling community, that they also needed to become ambassadors for Christ.

Another word for ambassador is missionary. The ambassador of a country goes as a representative of his nation into an alien situation and attempts to represent the commitments of his country in a foreign land. Paul reminded the Corinthians that this is the way it is with the church in mission. The newly planted Corinthian church was to celebrate and preserve the new unity which Jesus Christ was creating. They were also to move beyond themselves as ambassadors of Christ among neighbors and peoples who had not yet said "yes" to the new kingdom.

The joy and celebration of unity are not enough. The peace which we experience in being participants in the new community in Christ is not enough. There is always the call to move beyond. God, who experiences love within himself, reaches out in gentle, but vigorous, confrontational mission through his beloved Son. In the same way, the new congregation is to move constantly beyond the joy and grace and peace experienced in Christian community, to be ambassadors for Christ among persons who do not yet know him.

Acts Alive!

Most evangelical Christians have little difficulty believing the accounts of God's power as recorded in Acts and the four Gospels. The same persons, however, may find it incredulous to suppose that they can experience this same kind of power in church growth today. Believing that God has different plans for different periods of history, many sincere followers of Christ believe that with the availability of the written Scriptures, there is no need for a miraculous demonstration of God's power. We disagree!

Even as we write, there are alarming manifestations of growing satanic influence in all sectors of society. The sexual revolution has made a mockery of chastity and self-control within and outside the church, resulting in millions of unwanted pregnancies and the scourge of abortion on demand. An explosion of homosexual activity remains only somewhat checked by the advent of the deadly AIDS disease. Every form of pornographic media is readily available to those who lust after the emptiness of such sensual titillation.

There has been a tremendous growth of Eastern religions. New and strange cults, many of which are occult in nature, are multiplying. There has also been an increase of New Age religions, with a mix of traditional religion, psychology, self-improvement teaching, and occult power. Incidents of violent occult activity have increased in some countries, and especially in the United States. Some major U.S. cities have police divisions devoted to the investigations of occult-related homicides. Radio and television programs frequently feature persons who openly promote acts of sorcery and divination. Satan worship and witchcraft are common in many neighborhoods.

The American penchant for violence is nothing short of demonic in nature. The burgeoning national defense budget of the United States and the Soviet Union is a simple reflection of the tacit solution to every problem, as seen on a T-shirt: "Do unto others, before they do unto you." The current popularity of movies depicting or promoting violence as the solution to every domestic or foreign relations problem does not bode well for the future peace of the nations.

In the midst of all this darkness, there is some light. Especially in the United States, there is an unprecedented availability of Christian resources. Evangelistic personnel and programming are at an all-time high. And, by God's gracious hand, many churches around the world are growing. Lukewarm Christians are returning to the faith. New converts are coming to Christ.

However, there are relatively few persons coming to Christ who are truly secular in orientation. In the United States much of the widely touted current church growth is simply the "circulation of the saints" from one church to another. In other words, the same people are counted by more than one church as people move around. In some countries the growth is mostly through people leaving traditional religions to become Christians. Church growth has been generally slow among the other world religions or among secularists.

We believe that what is needed today is a demonstration of the kingdom of God as proclaimed and demonstrated in the book of Acts. We need God's acts among us today. For many of us, this will require a shift in worldview, as well as some radical changes in the way we preach, pray, and program for church growth.

There are five "versions" of the great commission in the Gospels and the book of Acts. Each of the commands to minister in Christ's name carries with it a power promise. Jesus did not send forth his disciples without the needed resources. And that power is still available today. Throughout history, God has moved with power when persons called upon him in sincere repentance, with hearts full of faith, longing for the fullness of God. Let us call on him in truth, expecting nothing less than an unprecedented move of God among us today.

So Let's Plant Churches

Eighty million people in North America have no relationship to the church. Only one third of our world of over five billion people profess to be Christian. Sixteen thousand people groups have no opportunity to say "yes" to the gospel, for there is little or no Christian witness among them. One and a half billion people live in nation-states committed to atheistic secularism. Eight hundred million Muslims are trying to convert the world. Half a billion people are hungry while modern nations pour a trillion dollars a year into arms.

As we see it, our world desperately needs a multiplication of clusters of redeemed people. We believe that every community, every city block, every language, every hamlet and village on earth deserves to have in its midst the signs of the kingdom of God which are present wherever two or three or more meet in Jesus' name. We believe there is no other hope for humankind, for we know there is salvation in no other name than that of Jesus.

Surely, there is no vocation, no enterprise, no vision, no commitment more precious to God. Surely, nothing is more significant to humanity than the multiplication of redeemed communities of people who love the Lord with all their mind, heart, and strength, and who also love their neighbors!

For Review, Study, and Discussion

1. Consider the idea that congregations are the centers for world mission. How might this concept affect the life of your church?

2. The book of Philippians is sometimes referred to as the "epistle of joy." Why might this be so?

3. What is the test of a disciple's faithfulness, as explained in this chapter? Do you agree with this assertion?

4. What should be the primary characteristic of the new communities Jesus is bringing together in church fellowships?

5. What does it mean to be an "ambassador" for Christ? How might this word picture help one to understand Christian mission?

Action Challenge

1. Think of at least one new frontier of ministry for your congregation. Commit yourself to pray about the possibilities for this new venture in outreach.

2. Ask another person in your fellowship about his or her vision for an expanded congregational outreach. Pray together for God's leading for further steps.

For Further Help

Out of the Saltshaker and into the World, by Rebecca Manley Pippert, InterVarsity Press, Downers Grove, Ill., 1979. A delightful description of approaches to faithful witness.

Bibliography

Administrative Guidelines for Church Planting, Eastern Mennonite Board of Missions, Salunga, PA 17538.

Balda, Wesley, *Heirs of the Same Promise*, Missionary Advanced Research and Communication Center, Monrovia, Calif., 1984.

Banks, Robert, *Paul's Idea of Community*, Eerdmans, Grand Rapids, Mich., 1980.

Bennis, Warren, and Nanus, Burt, *Leaders: The Strategies for Taking Charge*, Harper and Row, New York, 1985.

Bright, John, *The Kingdom of God: The Biblical Concept and Its Meaning for the Church*, Abingdon Press, Nashville, 1983.

Bryant, David, *With Concerts of Prayer: Christians Join for Spiritual Awakening and World Evangelization*, Regal Books, Ventura, Calif., 1984.

Change the World Ministries, P.O. Box 5838, Mission Hills, CA 91345.

Cho, Paul Y., *Prayer: Key to Revival*, Word Books, Waco, Tex., 1984.

Claerbaut, David, *Urban Ministry*, Zondervan, Grand Rapids, Mich., 1983.

Duewel, Wesley L., *Touch the World Through Prayer*, Francis Asbury Press, Grand Rapids, Mich., 1986.

Ellul, Jacques, *The Presence of the Kingdom*, Seabury Press, New York, 1967.

_____, *The Subversion of Christianity*, Eerdmans, Grand Rapids, MI, 1986.

Ensign, Grayson, and Edward Howe, *Bothered? Bewildered? Bewitched?* Recovery Publications, Cincinnati, Ohio, 1984.

Foster, John, *Church History, The First Advance*, Society for Promoting Christian Knowledge, London, England, 1972.

Foyle, Marjory F., *Overcoming Missionary Stress*, MARC, Europe, 1984.

Global Prayer Digest, U.S. Center for World Mission, 1605 Elizabeth Street, Pasadena, CA 91104 (818-797-1111).

Greenleaf, Robert K., *Servant Leadership*, Paulist Press, New York, 1977.

Henrichsen, Walter A., *Disciples Are Made, Not Born*, Victor Books, P.O. Box 1825, Wheaton, IL 60187.

Hopler, Thom, *A World of Difference*, InterVarsity Press, Downers Grove, Ill., 1981.

"How to Plant a Church Seminar," sponsored by Charles E. Fuller Institute of Evangelism and Church Growth, P.O. Box 91990, Pasadena, CA 91109.

Hummel, Charles, *Tyranny of the Urgent*, InterVarsity Press, Downers Grove, Ill., 1967.

Iverson, Dick, *Team Ministry*, Bible Temple Publications, Portland, Oreg., 1984.

Jacobs, Donald R., *Pilgrimage in Mission*, Herald Press, Scottdale, Pa., 1983.

Kraft, Charles H., *Communication Theory for Christian Witness*, Abingdon Press, Nashville, 1983.

—————, *Christianity in Culture*, Orbis Books, Maryknoll, 1979.

MacDonald, Gordon, and Thomas Nelson, *Restoring Your Spiritual Passion*, Oliver-Nelson, New York, 1986.

Meeks, Wayne, *The First Urban Christians*, Yale University Press, New Haven and London, 1983.

Newbigin, Lesslie, *Foolishness to the Greeks: The Gospel and Western Culture*, Eerdmans, Grand Rapids, Mich., 1986.

Nida, Eugene, and Charles R. Taber, *The Theory and Practice of Translations*, E. J. Brill, Leiden, 1969.

Niebuhr, H. Richard, *Christ and Culture*, Harper and Row, New York, 1951.

Operation World: Handbook for World Intercession. Available from Operation Mobilization, 121 Ray Avenue, Hawthorne, NJ 07506.

Ortiz, Juan Carlos, *Disciple*, Creation House, Carol Stream, IL 60187.

Peck, M. Scott, *People of the Lie*, Simon and Schuster, New York, 1983.

Pippert, Rebecca Manley, *Out of the Saltshaker and into the World*, InterVarsity Press, Downers Grove, Ill., 1979.

Richards, Lawrence O., and Clyde Hoeldtke, *A Theology of Church Leadership*, Zondervan, Grand Rapids, MI 49506.

Schaller, Lyle, *Looking in the Mirror: Self-Appraisal in the Local Church*, Abingdon Press, Nashville, 1984.

Sider, Ronald J., *Rich Christians in an Age of Hunger*, InterVarsity Press, Downers Grove, Ill., 1982.

Swindoll, Charles R., *Improving Your Serve*, Word Books, Waco, Tex., 1981.

Theissen, Gerd, *The Social Setting of Pauline Christianity*, Fortress Press, Philadelphia, 1982.

Tillapaugh, Frank R., *Unleashing the Church*, Regal Books, Ventura, Calif., 1983.

Training Faithful Men, produced by the Institute in Basic Youth Conflicts, Box 1, Oak Brook, IL 60521.

Wagner, Peter, *Your Spiritual Gifts Can Help Your Church Grow*, Regal Books, Ventura, Calif., 1979.

Wallis, Jim, *The Call to Conversion*, Harper and Row, San Francisco, 1981.

Watson, David, *Fear No Evil*, Harold Shaw, Wheaton, Ill., 1985.

Wimber, John, *Writing Your History in Advance*, Vineyard Ministries International, P.O. Box 1359, Placentia, CA 92670.

_____, *Power Evangelism*, Harper and Row, New York, 1986.

World Christian Prayer Map. Available from Change the World Ministries, P.O. Box 5838, Mission Hills, CA 91345.

Yoder, John Howard, *The Original Revolution*, Herald Press, Scottdale, Pa., 1972.

Scripture Index

The Authors

David Shenk   *Ervin R. Stutzman*

David Shenk grew up in the home of pioneer missionaries in Tanzania, where he was influenced by the East Africa revival. Recognizing the reality of God's grace on those mission efforts helped form his mission vision. David continues to have a deep desire to reach lost people with the gospel of salvation.

An Eastern Mennonite College graduate in biblical and social studies, David has also studied at New York University, where he acquired a doctorate in anthropology and religious studies education. He has authored a half-dozen books related to church history in Africa, the gospel and culture, and the gospel and world religions.

Although David has taught elementary through graduate school—both in the States and in Africa—his first calling and commitment is to pastoring, especially on the frontiers of evangelism. He and his wife, K. Grace Witmer, have always served on the frontiers of church planting and formation: in the mountain congregations during their college years in Virginia, during their two years of voluntary service in New York City as an alternative to military conscription, during their ten years in a Muslim country in Africa, and their six years in Nairobi. Now in suburban Lancaster, Pennsylvania, they are also helping to pastor a congregation which is experiencing good growth through evangelistic outreach. Their four children, Karen, Doris, Jonathan, and Timothy, have always supported their parents in the ministry.

During the 1980s David has been serving as director of home missions, and then overseas missions with a Mennonite mission board. This involvement has placed him in intimate contact with scores of church formation efforts, both in the United States and all the other five continents. He lives in the experience of cross-cultural church planting.

David has served as academic dean of Lithuania Christian College and as an Eastern Mennonite Missions consultant.

Ervin R. Stutzman was born as a twin in Kalona, Iowa, and lived there for three years. The family moved to Hutchinson, Kansas, after his father, Tobias, died in an automobile accident. He grew up as a member of the Amish Mennonite Church in that area, but affiliated in his later teenage years with the Mennonite church in Yoder, Kansas.

While attending Rosedale Bible Institute, he met Bonnie Haldeman, a member of a Church of the Brethren congregation near Lancaster, Pennsylvania. Shortly after their marriage, they served in Voluntary Service in Cincinnati, Ohio, with Rosedale Mennonite Missions. During his time in Cincinnati, Ervin directed the Voluntary Service household and served as an elder and later copastor of Mennonite Christian Assembly.

He also attended God's Bible College and Cincinnati Bible College and Seminary, earning a B.A. in Bible and Christian Ministries. He then studied communication at the University of Cincinnati, earning an M.A. in Communication Arts. He is presently pursuing his interest in communication on the Ph.D. level at Temple University in Philadelphia.

He moved to the Lancaster, Pennsylvania, area in 1982. Since then, he has worked as an associate director of Home Ministries of Eastern Mennonite Board of Missions, giving oversight and resourcing to church planting projects. After pastoring at Mount Joy Mennonite Church, he was called to be bishop of Landsdale District of the Lancaster Mennonite Conference. In this role, he has given oversight to a new church planting in his own district. Ervin's interests lie in the areas of preaching, teaching, and writing.

Ervin enjoys working together with his wife, Bonnie, on woodworking and house-remodeling projects. They have three children: Emma, Daniel, and Benjamin.

Ervin is dean of Eastern Mennonite Seminary in Harrisonburg, Virginia.